SIDE EFFECTS: WHAT CANDIDATES DON'T TELL YOU

TOMAS PAYNE

Finlee Augare Books (Chicago)

Finlee Augare Books, Chicago, IL
ISBN: 978-1-943080-25-0 (print)
ISBN: 978-1-943080-26-7 (e-book)
Library of Congress Control Number: 2016935377

Printed in the United States of America

TABLE OF CONTENTS

Introduction 1
Part 1: Billionaires 5
  Billionaire Wealth 5
  Fair Billionaire Income Tax 7
  Billionaire Estate Tax 10
  Billionaire Redistribution 12
  Say You Want A Revolution 15
  To Catch A Billionaire 18
  Billionaire Shell Game 20
  Top 3% & Why Care 22
  Billionaire Options 25
Part 2: Social Security 28
  Social Security Promises 28
  Social Security Unfairness 31
  Social Security Problems 33
  Social Security Solutions 36
Part 3: Healthcare/Medicare 43
  Evolution Of Healthcare 43
  Why Healthcare Costs Rise 46
  Other Healthcare Cost Drivers 49
  Medicare Broke 52
  Options To Fix Medicare 54
  Affordable Care Health Plan 57
  Healthcare Transparency 59
  Healthcare Options 61
  Single Payer Healthcare Pitch 65
  Single Payer Side-Effects 69
Part 4: Wages 71
  Income Inequality 71
Part 4: Wages 74
  Outsourcing 74

Depressed Wages 78
Minimum Wage 86
Minimum Wage & Business 89
Nationwide Minimum Wage 93
Minimum Wage Options 96
Part 5: Taxes 98
High Tax Rates 98
Increasing Taxes 100
History Of Cutting Taxes 105
Rational To Increase/Cut Taxes 109
Diminishing Returns Of Cutting Taxes 111
Capital Gains Tax 115
Dividend Tax 117
Tax Loopholes 119
Fair Share Of Taxes 123
Tax Proposals 126
Estate/Death Taxes 129
Part 6: Economics 133
Socialist Model 133
Socialist Experience 136
Capitalism & Entrepreneurialism 139
International Trade 143
Big Legal Awards 147
Conflict Of Interest 152
Wall Street Reform 155
Campaign Finance 158
Investing In Jobs 160
Myth Of Economic Growth 162
Part 7: Immigration 164
Immigration History 164
Immigration & Diversity 168
Immigration Implications 171
Deportation 175
Immigration Options 177
Part 8: World Myths 181
Nation Building In Middle East 181

Regime Change 185
War 187
Terrorism Background 189
Terrorism Issues 192
Middle East 194
Russia 196
China 199
China & Cyberwarfare 202
Part 9: Abrupt Climate Change 204
Climate Change History 204
Humans & Climate Change... 207
Climate Change Options 210
Real Cause Of Climate Change................................... 213
Energy 215
Part 10: Other 217
Gun Control.. 217
Postscript 221
Bibliography i
Author... end

INTRODUCTION

Isn't it about time for us to talk about issues based on facts and data instead of oft repeated mantras that take on a sacred quality?

These mantras are repeated phrases that may or may not have any basis in fact or reality but tend to sway our thinking. To say "There's no place like home" (from the Wizard of Oz) is harmless and based on valid experience. The statement that we only use 10% of our brains has been debunked, yet was the premise of a recent movie which was otherwise great fun. Political mantras, on the other hand, can be quite dangerous when they are based on false beliefs.

For those of us lucky enough to live in a democracy, we have elections every couple of years. Actually, the United States is a republic, since we elect representatives rather than have each voter show up in Washington to decide on every issue. If nothing else, there aren't enough hotels or even barns in Washington to house everyone. In lieu of that, our representatives create laws on our behalf, which gives them considerable power over us and significant incentive to covet positions in Washington.

In anticipation of elections, candidates promise us gorgeous beaches and forget to tell us about the sharks. They know that most people just want to be left alone to live their lives without fear of interference from outsiders, neighbors or the government.

Candidates take advantage of our distraction by coming to us every two to four to six years with sound bites, mantras, and pleas to get our votes. They appeal to our emotions rather than to our intellect since that is the quickest way to our hearts. Then many return to doing whatever they planned to do, hoping we won't peek behind the curtain to see what they're really up to. We get climate deniers and economic deniers, both of whom deny the facts. They should be embarrassed at being exposed, yet typically they are not.

We try to get them to tell us what they would actually do if we gave them the power, and what the side-effects would be. But candidates don't get elected by telling us the pain associated with their promises. Instead, they spin myths and withhold the effects of their plans as they promise us all gain and no pain.

In order for democracy to function well, it requires informed citizens who see through this bombardment of myths and misinformation. Unfortunately, some topics are hard to understand and may seem counter-intuitive. If you're looking for easy answers, there often aren't any, which is one of the most important things candidates don't tell us. They hope we won't dig.

So, let's peal back a few layers of the onion to see what's going on.

History doesn't repeat itself, but it does illustrate human behavior over time. If we choose not to learn from history, if we bury our heads, then we tend to repeat the mistakes of the past.

Here's a mantra: We live during tough times. Yet it was hard for the first immigrants who set foot on this land. It was dangerous for those on the wagon trains heading west. It was rough for the farmers when they left their homes and moved to the cities in search of work. We perceive our times as tougher because we're living through them and we don't know how this will turn out.

We tend to forget that America became great by individuals and groups overcoming adversity. Perhaps part of our angst comes from not having to face the clear hardships that our ancestors did, where there was no turning back. When they lost their jobs or the dustbowl took their farms, there was no safety net. They had to move on and do the best they could. Hardships gave their lives clarity and straightforward direction we often find lacking today. Few of us would want to return to what they faced but perhaps we can learn from their experiences.

It's true that today's events seem to happen faster than ever, yet is that any more disruptive than when our ancestors got on a boat, crossed the ocean, and faced an uncertain future in a new land? They did so because often they saw no better option. They were motivated to take personal risks. They plunged into uncertain futures.

Indeed, times have changed. We live in a global society with rapid communication that bombards us daily with terror and dismay. It tempts us with toys and wealth, if only …

Most Americans live much better than their counterparts 100 years ago, with indoor plumbing, air conditioning, refrigeration, vehicle transportation, cell phones, and countless appliances to make our lives easier. Yet, we are enticed to want more than we can afford, which leads us to despair. Our ancestors crossed oceans for less than we have today. Yet many of us today would not consider moving twenty miles for a better opportunity.

We lose faith in the future and become fearful, pining for a past shrouded in myth, a past that never was, when life was simpler and we didn't have the problems we face today. We the people look for answers while those who represent us announce that they have the cure to what ails us. In fact, they tell us that what ails us is what they have a solution to.

"Vote for me and I'll make your worries go away." *Just don't ask too many inconvenient questions.*

To collect our votes, many candidates appeal to our fears, hoping we'll see the world in their stark vision of black and white. It often sounds as if they're offering us a crystal clear choice in which we can sever our right hand or our left in order to serve their needs—to serve them instead of them serving us.

As an example, consider coal. Since coal is not a clean, green energy source, some people demand shutting down all coal production while others deny that there's a problem. Yet, if we think outside the box, there could be other choices, such as developing technologies to provide cleaner ways to use the coal we have.

Most of us believe that the ends do not justify the means. Americans believe in fairness and a prosperous future for our children. With regard to such broad goals for this country, we may not differ by as much as it seems, yet we argue over ways to get there. However, when the means lead to the wrong ends, the means necessarily must be wrong.

What I'm talking about are consequences. When a pharmacy fills a prescription, they provide a long list of side-effects, some of

Why haven't these greedy billionaires paid more taxes? Where are they hiding all their money?

These questions come about as a result of a misunderstanding of wealth and taxes. Bear with me for a moment.

To be clear, they aren't hiding their billions when Forbes reports on their wealth every year and increasingly there are disclosures of "hidden wealth" such as the Panama connection. We know who the billionaires are and how much they have. We even see their faces in the news.

Let's unravel the confusion on the connection between wealth and income taxes.

Wealth is a measure of how much a person's assets are worth. If you bought a house for $200,000 and it's now worth $300,000, you don't have any reportable income until you sell, yet your worth went up by $100,000. This works the same way for stocks, real estate, and businesses owned by the billionaires as it does for the middle-class and the poor.

If you were a small farmer living on your land, which had been in the family for generations, the land could be worth a million more than your family paid. You would be considered wealthier than your parents. The same goes for that antique car in your garage and the stack of old comic books in your attic. These all show you growing wealthier, but wealth is not cash or taxed until you sell your assets.

The billionaires are worth so much because the values of the companies they own, along with the stock and housing markets, have gone up, increasing the value of their assets. Yet no income is created until the assets are sold. It's important to understand this before we continue our discussion of the concentration of wealth.

FAIR BILLIONAIRE INCOME TAX

Candidates stump for our votes, pointing out that we have this billionaire crisis, referred to as a concentration of wealth. They repeatedly tell us (mantra) that we have to make the billionaires pay their fair share. So, help me understand this. Why is it that not one candidate making this claim offers even a single solution that would put a dent in this crisis during his/her term in office? Ask them!

You think this is BS. Then listen in.

Do you honestly believe that increasing income taxes on people making over $250,000 per year will hit the billionaire wealth concentration?

Think again.

Based on the IRS reports for 2013, the highest bracket they show contains 1,383 households with a minimum income of $45 million. That's one one-thousandth of one percent (0.001%) or one in 100,000 American households. This category includes 2.5 times the number of households in the billionaire club. But let's work with what we have. The total income for these households is $169 billion. They paid $41 billion in taxes or 24%.

If we target income over $45 million (so we're focused on the billionaires), that leaves us with $107 billion ($169 billion minus (1,383 households times $45 million each)). If all of this income belonged to the billionaires it would represent only 4% of their wealth. However, the number of billionaires represents only 40% of the number of households in this category. In addition, since

You're still welcome to support redistribution or not, but anyone who tells you this will solve your problems is hiding something, or more likely they're distracting you from the real problems.

SAY YOU WANT A REVOLUTION

For those people frustrated at getting shafted in this economy, calls for redistributing wealth from the billionaires sound tempting. The entire idea of wealth concentration runs counter to our democratic values. Except, don't forget that our Founding Fathers were wealthy by colonial standards. George Washington was at one time the largest landowner in the colonies.

As you get stirred out of anger and frustration to support candidates who call for revolution, be careful what you ask for.

The United States was birthed in revolution. It was an inspiring act, a product of the Enlightenment, a creation of a new society that welcomed tens of millions of refugees and turned into the greatest economy in the world. Perhaps because of that, there's a romantic nostalgia for revolutions to fix what ails America today.

But when people talk about "revolution" today, consider the history of revolutions. Let us not forget that the representatives sent to Philadelphia in 1776 were initially charged with airing grievances with Britain, not declaring independence. Yet, they and their supporters in the state legislatures took it upon themselves to declare independence in rebellion against government control thousands of miles away.

The war turned brother against brother, revolutionaries vs. loyalists, foreshadowing the Civil War of the next century. The war lasted eight long years during which American forces lost most of the battles. It was only by the intervention of the French fleet at

Yorktown that the revolutionaries won and were able to form a new nation.

The government that formed under the Constitution looked nothing like the Articles of Confederation that had bound the colonies during the war. It contained a stronger central government than what the people had wanted in large part to deter Britain and others from interfering with the new nation. The end looked much different than what the people expected at the time of the Declaration of Independence.

Throughout the history of the world, successful revolutions have been few and success is open to interpretation. The French Revolution deposed an autocratic king. That led to the Reign of Terror that even took the lives of the leaders of the revolution. The chaos led to the rise of Napoleon. He stirred up the people with pride, which he used in his attempt to conquer all of Europe. Napoleon lost some half a million men in his failed military campaign against Russia. He was defeated and exiled. In the end, a king was returned to the throne.

The Russian revolution deposed a tsar and brought democracy—for a few months. Then the Bolsheviks took over. Stalin brought repression and his own reign of terror that killed millions of his own citizens. The Cuban Revolution removed a dictator who exploited his people. The regime that replaced the dictator repressed those same people with dashed hopes.

The revolution in Libya didn't go well. The rebellion in Syria is a disaster. Many other revolutions have been attempted. Few succeeded. Rarely did the result measure up to the announced intentions. They all fell victim to side-effects and unintended consequences.

Revolutions encounter conflicting objectives from those who foment revolution. However, the big problem is that, after revolutionaries dispose of the wealthy people, the wealth vanishes. That leaves little to solve the problems of the people. For example, during and after the Russian Revolution, stocks and businesses held by the wealthy became worth much less. After all, value is a measure of what a willing buyer would pay and there weren't any willing buyers. The same goes for the real estate and art.

This is the dirty little secret of revolutions that promise redistribution of wealth. Remember, of all the revolts and revolutions mentioned above, only the American Revolution was not about redistributing wealth. It was about severing ties with a country across the ocean.

Thus, when people talk of revolution today, be wary of motives and of what history tells us about the disconnect between promises and results.

TO CATCH A BILLIONAIRE

As demonstrated elsewhere, income taxes and estate taxes will do little to reduce the concentration of wealth. Revolutions rarely turn out well for the people. Is there anything else we can consider to reduce the concentration of wealth?

We could adopt a wealth tax as some states have done over the years. That would be an annual tax on the value of assets. It wouldn't hurt billionaires who would lobby for exemptions or move to a less tax burdened country. It would hurt those less fortunate than the billionaires as well as small businesses who have been the engine of job growth. Are fewer jobs a fair price to pay for a reduced concentration of wealth by adopting this tax?

There has to be a way. In fact there is.

If the idea of billionaires bothers you to the point you have to do something, buy less of their products and services. If you stop giving them money, they will have less wealth. It's that simple. The popular companies they own will have less revenues and profits. That will reduce the value of their assets and hit them where it hurts.

That means no longer buying popular products and services at affordable prices from popular outlets that we've come to depend on. It also means no longer using our usual social media outlets or supporting many of our favorite sports teams. Doing without or paying higher prices elsewhere are small prices to pay to reduce the concentration of wealth, isn't it? But if you shift your buying to smaller companies, you will be launching a different group of billionaires.

To avoid that, you could grow your own food, make your own clothes, build your own house, and turn off your sources of entertainment. Because chances are, whenever you buy from a big company, a billionaire benefits. Even certain entertainers are moving up toward the billionaire class.

Let's say you do become independent in order to stop the billionaires. One of the nasty side effects will be that tens of millions of jobs would vanish as affected companies cut back because of lower sales. Any remaining pension plans would fail. 401k and other retirement plans would become worth much less. In fact, if enough Americans become self-sufficient, there would be no income and thus no tax revenue to support Social Security, Medicare or other government programs.

At least the billionaires would have less.

In other words, this would be worse than Russian roulette since in that game, you stand a chance of surviving.

The point of this discussion is not to defend the billionaires. Rather, let's recognize that each and every one of us willingly gave many of them that wealth as we chose their products and services over more expensive or less desirable alternatives. If we had not, they wouldn't be on the billionaire list.

For those people still upset with the billionaires, why keep buying from them?

Having said that, one category of billionaires does not produce a recognizable product or service. While over half of the top 200 billionaires acquired and/or currently hold their wealth in products and services we all use, there are 30 hedge fund/investment billionaires who do not. They made their money in stocks and real estate as market values went up.

BILLIONAIRE SHELL GAME

Who are they kidding when candidates say the billionaires should pay more yet the proposals they put forth would have minimal effect on billionaire wealth concentration or the wellbeing of everyday Americans? And, if these candidates talking about the billionaires aren't really going after the billionaires, then who are they targeting and why?

Here's what doesn't make sense. If billionaires are the problem, then why don't these candidates sit down with that one family whose wealth exceeds that of the bottom 130 million Americans and jawbone them into contributing more to help out? If these candidates want to target billionaires, why not raise their specific taxes? Why bother the rest of us with 70,000 pages of tax regulations that only such a wealthy family could understand? Part of the answer is that, with all their resources, such a family can figure out how to avoid the taxes all those regulations were intended to collect.

Yet candidates who rail against the billionaires are adamant that all billionaires must contribute more. Okay, there are 536 American billionaires according to the Forbes report. It's not as if the government doesn't know where to find them. Why not approach these individuals who represent the most wealth concentration?

Alas, these candidates are not satisfied with the billionaires. "Make the billionaires pay," is a clever mantra, but billionaires are merely convenient figureheads to rile up their supporters to go to the polls and give them power.

So when candidates get done pointing to all that wealth concentration in the hands of billionaires and get their supporters riled up, where do they look to fix the problem? They go after the one-percenters, which according to the IRS includes households with taxable income in excess of $428,713 in 2013. Then these candidates set the bar at $250,000, which the Census Bureau tells us includes the top 3% of all American households.

Somehow in a government awash in $19 trillion of debt (that's with a "T"), there doesn't appear to be any difference between billions and $250,000. That is modern political math.

For comparison, the IRS shows that for 2013 the 1% category (1.4 million households) starts at $428,713, the 0.1% bracket (140,000 households) starts at $1,860,848, and the 0.01% group (14,000 households) starts at $9,460,540.

Why don't these candidates go after the billionaires? That's easy. Billionaires have options. They have lawyers, accountants, and lobbyists to help them create, find, and use loopholes to avoid paying whatever "soak-the-rich" taxes Washington might come up with. Failing that, if the government raises their tax rates high enough, they'll take their wealth elsewhere.

The candidates who call for taxing the rich know this.

The French recently got a lesson on raising taxes on their wealthy when they increased the top income tax rate to 75%. They calculated how much additional revenue would come rolling in and received half of what they expected. They forgot that tax policy provides incentives to change taxpayer behavior.

Every time "soak-the-rich" taxes are increased, the upper middle class pays the price while the billionaires find a way out. This is convenient for these candidates since it allows them to keep their "Make the billionaires pay," mantra. The image of billionaires will always remain as ready targets and as a rationale to argue for more tax increases on the upper middle class, a tacit wink-wink, nod-nod.

If the target is billionaire wealth, then focus on the billionaires instead of those much less fortunate, but don't be disappointed when you achieve your goal and the results don't meet expectations.

TOP 3% & WHY CARE

Why should we care about 3% upper middle class taxpayers that the redistributionists target?

For one, there's high turnover in and out of this group. Looking at incomes above $1 million from the Tax Foundation, only half of the individuals who reached this level did so more than once in a 9 year period. Only 6% of the individuals who reached this at least once remained at this level for the full 9 years. The number of people who qualified between 2001 and 2010 ranged from 169,000 to 392,000. Turnover also takes place in the incomes above $250,000 (the 3%).

Looking at the $200,000 plus category from the US Census Bureau, 5.6% of all U.S. households reached this level in 2014. But wait. This category also included:

- 7.5% for family households
- 9.0% for those aged 45-54 (the high income years)
- 10.6% for households with four family members
- 10.7% for households with bachelor's degrees
- 10.9% for households with two or more earners

Applying these results to the $250,000 and above category implies that while 3% of all households qualify at any time, that could be 6% for households with two or more earners, and even higher for those who hit this category at least once during their lifetimes. In other words, if you're young and single, your chances of hitting this top earner category at some point in your life are much higher than what certain candidates would like you to believe.

Why do these candidates point to billionaires and then raise taxes on those making $250,000? Sales sharks call it bait and switch. Magicians call it sleight of hand. Candidates call it the moral right thing to do.

They do it because it's easier to get people riled up over the billionaires than to explain that your neighbors and possibly you may be lucky enough to move up and get hit with the soak-the-rich tax at $250,000. In addition, those who slip in and out of this category are made to feel guilty on behalf of the billionaires. It's all part of the wink-wink game.

It's also a reflection that while there are 1.4 million one-percenters and about 3.8 million making over $250,000, there are only 14,000 of the 0.01% group that represents the true concentration of wealth and income. Yet, even with their high per capita incomes, they only represent 4.3% of total incomes because there are only 14,000 of them. While it might feel satisfying to do so, even taxing them 100% would not cover the Federal budget deficit. There just aren't enough of them.

Like the old joke about why rob a bank—that's where the money is, these candidates have figured out that there is five times as much income in households earning $250,000 to $9 million as there is in households above that level since there are some 250 times as many of them.

Why don't these candidates fess up? Just say they're going to soak the upper middle class rather than baiting us with the 536 billionaires and raising taxes on those who, through hard work and some luck make it to $250,000.

Who are the people who earn between $250,000 and $1 million that we should care? They include lawyers and doctors, and quite a few small business people who own the shops, restaurants, and dealerships, the owner of the McDonalds franchise down the street, and the owner of the plumbing company that fixes your plumbing needs.

When these candidates say "Look at those billionaires," recognize there are only about 536 of them. Forbes publishes a list, making them easy to identify. It should be easy to focus your efforts on them. If they say "Look at those greedy hedge-fund operators," then focus on them. Many of them are in the 0.01% group with incomes above $9 million.

If instead, they decide to tax the $250,000 group, recognize they're going after the 3% today that likely will include over 6% during our lifetimes. These are the people who achieved the American dream and climbed a little above, perhaps for one time in their lives. If you're young, this group very well could include you down the road or your children.

BILLIONAIRE OPTIONS

If, after all the discussion on billionaires, certain candidates still want to redistribute wealth because they don't want a billionaire class and would prefer to live in a country with more equal wealth distribution, what are their options?

1. **Increase income taxes**. This will hurt those one-percenters not rich enough to play the billionaire game. As demonstrated, it will have minimal effect on billionaire wealth distribution since very little of that wealth goes through income (see Billionaire Wealth).
2. **Increase estate taxes**. This will hurt those below the billionaires who are not wealthy enough to play the billionaire game. Billionaires have two options to avoid estate taxes. First is the marital deduction. Second is the charitable deduction. They can set up charitable foundations as many billionaires have and donate their estate to their own foundation instead of paying estate taxes. To the extent they are taxed on the balance of their estates, it will be after they die, which will take a generation to flush out the wealth from the current generation of billionaires. Set at the right level, this could address the inherited wealth issue without destroying small businesses upon the death of their owners.
3. **Create an annual wealth tax**. This will hurt those below the billionaires who are not wealthy enough to play the

game. Billionaires can move their assets outside the country or renounce citizenship to avoid this tax.

4. **Revolution and redistribution**. As discussed under Say You Want a Revolution, revolutions rarely turn out the way their leaders say it will or to the benefit of the people. Oh, the leaders will promise redistribution, but there are two ways that turns out. First, everyone gets a one-time check for $6,250 and that's the end of the revolution. More likely, the leaders of the revolution grab the money for themselves so they can hold onto power. They may redistribute some of the money, but when they realize there isn't enough to go around, they will need a military guard and to pay off supporters in order to stay in power. In essence, the people will trade one entitled class for another.
5. **Stop buying from companies owned by billionaires**. That is the quickest way to redistribute wealth. The inconvenient side-effect will be higher prices and lower quality products. Why? Product-and-service-related billionaires got their wealth by providing products and services that we all use. However, this won't affect the hedge fund and investment billionaires. It will also cut employment, hurting millions of poor and middle-class Americans.
6. **Target hedge funds**. Proposals that target hedge funds include increasing the capital gains tax, applying a Wall Street transaction tax, and removing the "carried-interest."
    a) Increasing the capital gains tax will hurt hedge fund operators. It will also hurt many other individuals with the inflation tax (see Capital Gains). Actually, tying the capital gains tax to inflation and then using the ordinary tax rate on real gains would fully tax the hedge fund operators who rarely own companies for very long.
    b) Applying a Wall Street transaction tax will hit the computerized automated transactions. For the most part, these are not hedge funds but a different class of financial players. Most of the hedge funds buy and sell businesses over a short time period (1-5 years), not

necessarily through the stock exchanges. Thus, the transaction tax may not affect them.

c) Removing the "carried interest" would hurt the employees of hedge funds more than the owners. The employees often receive stock options and other grants that they don't have to pay much or anything for. As such, they have no risk in the investment and any gain is really a form of salary and bonus. The owners have invested their own money. Their gains are capital gains in the same way any asset sale can create such a gain. Thus, changing the "carried-interest" won't hurt the hedge-fund owners as much as it will hit their employees.

7. Not to be facetious, but the quickest way to ensure you're living in a society with more equal distribution of wealth and income is to move to such a country. Many immigrants are doing just that when they move to the United States and Europe. Many of them come from countries with even worse income distribution than in the United States.
8. Become a billionaire or at least wealthy by providing goods and services that other people want. That's how the entrepreneurs who built the tech companies did it.
9. Recognize that the focus on billionaires as the source of our problems is a smoke-screen. Even if we took all their billions, it wouldn't solve poverty, depressed wages, or any of the other social issues we face. Candidates focus on billionaires because it's an easier sound-bite for them than to address our real problems and it diverts our attention from the side-effects of their plans.

Thus, the angst over the billionaire class provides a great rallying cry to those offended by such concentration of wealth. It feeds their anger and increasing tax rates makes people feel as if they're doing something. The reality is that wealth concentration does not yield to easy solutions.

Now certain candidates want to increase the retirement age and raise taxes to keep Social Security solvent. How is this right, fair, or ethical?

To make matters worse, the government in 1956 added disability benefits to the plan without increasing payroll taxes enough to pay for these benefits. Disability income has from the beginning been a welfare transfer program, paid by current workers to current beneficiaries.

Rather than increasing payroll taxes enough to cover disability benefits, the government grabbed money from the retirement plan trust fund to cover disability costs. No attempt was made to collect enough taxes to build a trust fund to cover future disability benefits, in part because unlike retirement benefits, disability costs are difficult to estimate. Whenever the economy goes into recession and jobs are lost, more disabled workers claim disability benefits. This causes the government to dig deeper into the Social Security "trust fund" and puts all of Social Security at risk.

SOCIAL SECURITY UNFAIRNESS

The Social Security "trust fund" is running out of money, so who shall we get to pay for it?

Upon hearing that the "trust" will run out of funds, certain candidates call for raising payroll taxes on the "rich" and taking away their benefits. This would turn Social Security from the initial intent of a funded retirement plan like a pension, into another social welfare entitlement plan, a wealth transfer from the "rich" to the poor.

First, let's clarify that the "rich" for the purpose of raising payroll taxes include anyone who makes over $118,500 per year. That includes 18% of American households in any given year and many more who will visit this group during their working careers.

Some candidates complain that billionaires don't pay any more into Social Security than those who pay the maximum payroll tax each year ($118,500). Yet billionaires also don't receive a penny more, either.

In fact, the calculation of Social Security benefits is regressive (though some call it progressive), in that:

- The first $10,272 in annual income subject to payroll taxes will create benefits at 90% of what was earned over 35 years.
- The next $51,612 of income (to $61,884) receives benefits at 32%.

- Any income over $61,884 up to $118,500 receives benefits of 15%.

Thus, Social Security already significantly benefits the poor at the expense of the middle class and the rich. Stated another way:

- Anyone whose lifetime earnings (over 35 years) averaged $10,272 would receive 90% of their working earnings during retirement, some three times what they and their employers paid in.
- Anyone who averaged $61,884 over their lifetimes would receive a blended 42% of their earnings in benefits or 37% more than they and their employers paid in.
- Those who earn at or above the payroll tax maximum of $118,500 would receive a blended 29% benefit of the payroll tax maximum, which is close to what they and their employers paid in.

In other words, the top group is the only one that pays for their retirement benefits through their payroll taxes, and they are often subject to income taxes on their benefits.

Already, all except the top group are getting an amazing retirement benefit with Social Security, while the top group is only getting their money back. However, there are candidates who want to make the retiree contract even worse. These candidates want to reduce or eliminate the already lower benefit rate for those 18% of Americans who are at or above $118,500 by applying a means test and raising the maximum applicable for payroll taxes.

In short, after the government has spent the money, these candidates want to take Social Security away from the only group that has paid their own way. That must be a new definition of fairness.

SOCIAL SECURITY PROBLEMS

For decades, people said that Social Security was rushing toward insolvency. If so, what's the problem and how did we get here?

First, people are living longer and collecting more benefits than were anticipated when Social Security was set up. Some people point out that in the 1930s life expectancy at birth was 60 years and the retirement age was set out at 65. Yet, this doesn't tell the entire story. There was still high childhood mortality in the 1930s.

In 1940, when the program was getting started, only 57% of the population that reached age 21 made it to age 65. At age 65, life expectancy during retirement was 13.7 years. By 1990, more of the 21-year-olds made it to age 65 (78%) as seen in the chart below and life expectancy during retirement was 17.5 years, almost 4 years longer.

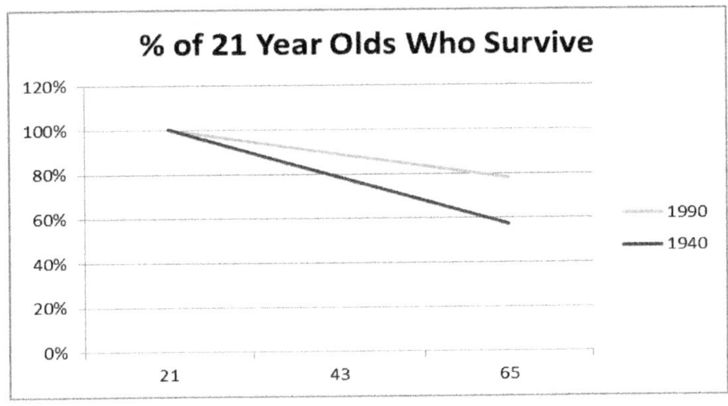

SOCIAL SECURITY SOLUTIONS

How do we tackle Social Security so that it doesn't leave retirees without the benefits they've paid for?

For the American people, when our personal budgets are out of whack, we have several choices. We can earn more, spend less or we can take on more debt, bury our heads in the sand, and pray we win the lottery. There is no lottery big enough to come up with the trillions of dollars the government needs. Here are our options:

1. **Do nothing and keep kicking the can down the road**: The government has done this for decades. Many of our current officeholders will be gone before this issue becomes so critical it can no longer be deferred. This seems to be the preferred solution for those who can't face up to the cost of fixing this problem and can't lead us through the complex issues. Remember, candidates don't survive by telling us what their plans will cost.
2. **Privatize**: For those who believe the government has mismanaged the program and can't be trusted to fix it, privatizing is a solution.
    - One option would have the government invest the "trust fund" balance from payroll taxes collected today for tomorrow's benefits in the stock and bond market as is done for pension plans. After the meltdown in 2008, this doesn't sound very appealing to most Americans. In addition, doing this would put the government in the role of owning trillions of dollars'

worth of American companies, which would radically change markets and the entire free enterprise system. Government ownership of the means of production runs counter to American entrepreneurial values, and in fact has failed in places like the Soviet Union and Communist China.

- Another option would be to let younger workers keep a portion of their payroll taxes in personal accounts they control and can pass on to their kids. The upside would be that they would hold the account so that the government couldn't spend their retirement funds elsewhere. With prudent investment, they could get a better retirement package than what the government is offering. While this would benefit the savvy and people wealthy enough to hire professionals to manage their money, most people don't have the knowledge, discipline or patience to save and invest their own funds and deal with market risk.
- Those who most ardently promote privatization have the resources and discipline to make this work. For many Americans there would remain the risk that they would reach retirement penniless. We all lose as a society when some of us face poverty in our retirement years. Aside from the human cost, we lose in terms of subsidized healthcare, subsidized long term care, and other resources for those who are no longer able to contribute in the workplace to pay their own way.
- Besides, privatizing doesn't deal with the unfunded nature of current Social Security obligations/promises and the fact the government has already spent the money.

3. Increase the retirement age:
   - Those who support increasing the retirement age argue that effective retirement longevity has gone up 5 years since Social Security was created. Either tax rates have to go up or benefits have to come down, including a higher retirement age.
   - Increasing the retirement age would take into

consideration how people are living longer. For those born in 1960 and after, the retirement age has already been increased to 67. Increasing the full retirement age to 68, 69, or 70 would reduce the amount of money the government needs to fund Social Security.

- Those who oppose an increase argue that doing so will hurt lower and middle income individuals who depend more on Social Security and may find it difficult to find and keep a job at ages 68-70. Despite anti-discrimination laws, it has been difficult for senior citizens to get good-paying jobs as they get up in years. Often they have health issues that would qualify them for disability benefits if they can't collect retirement benefits. That would defeat the purpose of increasing the retirement age.
- If a decision is made to change the retirement age, then the question is where to place the cutoff. It would seem unfair to apply this to anyone over the age of 50, since they are approaching retirement and have been planning their lives around the current guidelines. The argument could also be made that those over the age of 45 have already contributed a significant amount in payroll taxes toward their own retirements to have the goalpost moved out again.
- The other consideration is that increasing the age will push more senior citizens into the workplace, blocking jobs for younger workers. This will tend to depress wages as more workers chase fewer jobs. Unlike what candidates would have us believe, there is no free lunch.

4. Reduce annual cost-of-living adjustments:
   - The government uses the CPI-W (consumer price index-urban wage earners and clerical workers) to determine the annual inflation increase in Social Security benefits.
   - Individuals who seek to change this argue that this index doesn't reflect the true cost of inflation since it doesn't reflect changes in buying habits over time. For example, today's appliances are more energy efficient

than in the past. These people propose using the "chained CPI," which corrects for these biases.

- Those who argue against this change note that it would result in lower annual increases by 0.25-0.30% per year. Over 30 years, that could amount to 9% lower benefits.
- Which approach is right? No one wants lower benefits. Those who want this change have a point in that technology has improved our lives in ways that are not reflected in the CPI-W, which uses the same basket of purchases for decades. Thus, CPI-W tends to overstate inflation.
- Those who argue against this change note that some changes in habits distort the picture. If you were used to eating beef twice a week and beef prices doubled, you might switch to chicken. The "chained CPI" would ignore the beef increase and assume you would continue to eat chicken instead of beef. In this way, the "chained CPI" tends to understate inflation.
- The math can be complicated, but the simple answer is that both arguments have merit and neither measure of inflation reflects the reality of a retiree's finances.

5. Reduce the benefit formula:
    - The current formula for determining retirement benefits takes the average, inflation adjusted earnings over the highest 35 year work period. Then the first so many dollars get 90% benefit. The next so many dollars gets 32% benefit. The balance gets 15% benefit. Like the income tax brackets, the cutoffs are adjusted each year for inflation.
    - Since the lower income brackets leave a retiree at or below the poverty levels, it would be unthinkable to reduce the rates on the first and probably the second brackets.
    - Doing so on the upper bracket is problematic since these are the only people who cover their benefits through payroll taxes. In addition, reducing the 15% benefit rate would hurt the middle class already hurting from stagnant wages.

> bank and when you went to take it out, the bank told you that you were doing well and they didn't have to give you back your money? That's what these candidates are saying.

Despite the difficulty of dealing with Social Security, it's time to address the issues instead of passing the problems on to the next generation.

PART 3: HEALTHCARE/MEDICARE

EVOLUTION OF HEALTHCARE

Why have healthcare costs skyrocketed over the past 50 years?

Many theories have been put forth centered around greed and big corporate oligopolies. First, let's look at how we got here.

Up until the 1930s, people had to pay for their own medical costs. If they didn't have cash, they bartered with their local doctors or did without. As late as 1950, healthcare costs represented only 4.3% of GDP as compared to 17.5% today.

Several things happened during the Great Depression and afterwards that altered healthcare delivery and its costs.

1. During the Great Depression, hospitals worried that declining revenues would force them to close. In response, they created service plans that collected premiums from large companies and schools in exchange for promises of service. In 1946, the American Hospital Association commission took the name Blue Cross.
2. Also during the Depression, doctors worried about their incomes. Working through the American Medical Association, they created their own plans, which in 1946 became Blue Shield. Later, Blue Cross and Blue Shield merged into one of the premier healthcare insurance providers in the United States.
3. Watching the success of Blue Cross and Blue Shield, other

insurance providers got into the healthcare insurance business after World War II.

4. During World War II, the government put into effect wage controls at a time when young men were going into military service, leaving a shortage of labor to support the military buildup. In order to attract labor while not being able to increase wages, businesses offered company paid health insurance. Government agencies decided to allow the additional fringe benefits as not violating wage controls since at that time, the IRS did not consider health insurance as taxable wages. The fact that healthcare costs were low factored into that decision. This was important because businesses could deduct insurance premiums on their income taxes while employees didn't have to pay taxes on the benefit. With 40-52% corporate tax rates at that time, this was a considerable incentive. Using this tax advantage, businesses expanded the use of healthcare insurance as a tool to attract workers.
5. During and after the war, government policy decisions enabled unions to bargain for healthcare benefits as part of collective bargaining. This brought the number of union workers covered by such plans from under a million in 1946 to almost 30 million workers and dependents by 1954.
6. The availability of advanced medical technology blossomed after the war, with penicillin (1946), other antibiotics like streptomycin (1943), open-heart surgery (1952), kidney transplant (1954), heart pacemaker (1957), measles vaccine (1963), heart transplant (1967), and the list goes on. This is important since new technologies meant more drugs and procedures and higher healthcare costs, which in turn increased demand for group healthcare insurance.
7. In 1965, Medicare and Medicaid were adopted as extensions to Social Security.

The net effect of all of these developments was that by 2006, employer-based healthcare plans increased to cover 162 million people. Seventeen percent of the population was covered by public programs, and individual plans covered another 7%. In addition, 55 million Americans are covered under Medicare. Compare this to 1940 when only 9% of Americans had any form of healthcare plan.

Today, we all recognize the importance of healthcare insurance when total healthcare costs amount to 17.5% of GDP. But why is this history important to understanding our current high costs?

For the answer, look back at items 1 and 2 above. Healthcare insurance first and foremost benefits the providers: hospitals, physicians, clinics, drug companies, and healthcare service providers. It provides them with a steady source of income. It provides insurance to them so they get paid whether or not the patient can afford the treatments.

In a nutshell, all forms of group insurance benefit the big company healthcare providers. In addition, government policies during and after World War II have fostered this trend.

WHY HEALTHCARE COSTS RISE

So what if big healthcare companies benefit from group insurance. Workers, retirees, and other Americans benefit as well. What's the problem?

The problem is that while the companies and those covered by group plans are winners, there are losers in this healthcare game.

The biggest side-effect of group healthcare plans is higher costs. The losers are all Americans affected by higher healthcare costs, by employer reaction to these costs, and by tax increases to pay for higher medical costs. Employer reactions include 1) layoffs when costs get too high, 2) lower wages to offset higher medical costs since employers look at the total cost not just wages. Thus, this burden affects all Americans.

Why does group insurance lead to higher costs?

What group healthcare plans and Medicare have in common is that they shift the burden for paying the majority of healthcare costs from the individual patient to an institution that pools costs, either Medicare/Medicaid or healthcare insurance companies. This weakens any incentive for consumers/patients and providers to consider the most cost-effective way to administer healthcare.

How?

These plans separate patients from the true cost of the healthcare they obtain. Patients and their families are often only on the hook for 20% of their healthcare costs with annual caps for out-of-pocket expenditures.

Why is this important?

Imagine the auto industry adopting this type of plan. Don't worry about tipping them off. They already know how to play the game in a slightly different way.

Under this hypothetical plan, when you went in to buy a car, you only had to pay 20% with an annual cap of $10,000. Before the plan, you could buy a Toyota Corolla for $18,000 or a high-performance BMW for $100,000. With the plan, you pay $3,600 (20% of $18,000) for the Corolla and $10,000 for the BMW (limited to the cap). How many people would be tempted to buy the pricier car for a little more money?

Realizing that consumers only pay 20% or less, the auto industry in this world would be tempted to increase the price of the Corolla so the consumer would have to pay $5,000 and increase the price of the BMW, since the individual consumer wouldn't have to pay a penny more. The buyer might grumble about paying a little more for the Corolla, but this might encourage buyers to trade up. All of a sudden, car prices would go through the roof.

This would be a big boon for the auto industry which would receive higher prices. Consumers would get fancier cars for less than they pay now. What's not to like?

Don't forget the auto buyer premiums everyone would have to pay for this plan. With vehicle costs going up as a result of the 20% factor, the premiums have to go up as well, meaning that everyone is paying for this scheme.

In the healthcare case, all Americans pay the additional group cost through: 1) higher income taxes to cover Medicare deficits, 2) higher prices to cover business medical insurance premiums, and 3) higher unemployment when medical costs make the cost of employing American workers too high.

This disconnect of patients only paying a portion of their medical costs has meant that consumers aren't as cost conscious when they get medical services as when they buy other goods and services. It means that patients are more willing to get unnecessary procedures, such as cosmetic mole removal, instead of only procedures with medical necessity. It also means that when doctors and hospitals add services and procedures, patients don't fight back as hard. After all, patients often are paying 20% or less with an annual cap.

This has encouraged healthcare providers to increase their prices, push more services, and to bury their fees in tons of paperwork while working directly with insurance companies. Consumers often don't see the cost of their healthcare until after the insurance company has paid their portion.

In my area, one MRI clinic charges double what others in the area charge. When asked why, they said this is how the game is played.

OTHER HEALTHCARE COST DRIVERS

What else is driving up healthcare costs?

Large malpractice lawsuits hit the news from time to time, including some $85 billion since 1990. Those who support the current tort system, including the one-percenter attorneys who make millions, say we need a way to punish wrong-doers and to compensate victims.

On the surface, that makes sense, except as will be noted under Big Legal Awards the current tort system fails in this regard. Victims should be compensated for actual wrongs committed against them. Yet, there is a difference between actual damages and punitive damages that turn the courts into a lottery win for the lawyers as much as the victims.

There are two side-effects of these tort lawsuits.

Big settlements get paid out of malpractice insurance. That leads those insurance companies to increase premiums not only for the party concerned but for all healthcare providers. Those providers then have to cover their costs by increasing prices to consumers. Most of that increase gets paid by medical insurance companies. Those companies then have to increase insurance premiums paid by businesses, consumers, and taxpayers. Thus, we all pay for the settlement shared by the attorney and the victim.

It doesn't stop there. The risk of malpractice suits pressures hospitals and doctors to perform unnecessary medical tests and procedures intended to protect them, not the patients. Not only do they not want to deal with even higher malpractice insurance premiums, they don't want the negative publicity of having missed something. More tests and procedures translate into higher healthcare costs for all of us and get passed through medical insurance premiums. As an aside, additional procedures benefit healthcare providers with additional work, revenue, and income, so they lack the incentive to curb these practices.

Another cost driver of higher medical costs is breakthroughs in new and expensive technologies for diagnosis and treatment. Whereas in other industries technology improves productivity and provides better products and/or lower costs, in healthcare, the more we can do, the more procedures we do.

To support the demand for additional MRI, PET, and other equipment, medical institutions set up facilities. After they do, they need to fill up equipment schedules to pay for their investment. This dovetails with the pressure to do more tests in order to avoid the embarrassment and the cost of having missed something, no matter how obscure. After all, more procedures means more profit, while missing something means added costs that have to be passed on.

Adding to this trend, medical groups bring doctors and test facilities together so that doctors have a vested interest in using expensive technologies from a financial standpoint as well as to prevent lawsuits. Insurance programs pay the bulk of the costs so that patients don't feel the pressure to resist. Meanwhile, the medical establishment and insurance companies keep the billing and necessity of procedures complicated so most patients don't know how to argue.

What has become perhaps the biggest driver of higher costs is healthcare industry consolidation. Over the past few decades, the healthcare payers have grown into a few very large players including Medicare and the large corporate health insurance companies. To deal with rising costs, Medicare and the big insurance companies have pushed back. The government has pushed more regulation to control an industry that has reached 17.5% of the entire U.S. economy.

Healthcare providers have responded to this increased pressure from big Medicare/Insurance. Big hospitals have acquired smaller ones, setting up conglomerates. Small medical clinics and independent doctors are unable to deal with all of the complex rules and pressure to negotiate lower fees. To compensate they have joined with hospitals and other major medical groups. This healthcare consolidation gives hospitals and doctors more clout to stand up to the demands from Medicare and the insurance industry, and to handle increased reporting requirements and regulations.

Medicare and the big insurance companies have encouraged this trend with their practices. It's easier for the government (Medicare) to only have to deal with a few healthcare providers. That makes it easier for them to regulate and negotiate. It also means less competition.

Big encourages bigger. It's also easier for huge healthcare providers to deal with huge insurance companies, Medicare, and governmental regulations, particularly the thick volume called the Affordable Care Act (ACA). By its actions, the government through ACA is encouraging bigness and consolidation so they have fewer private sector players to deal with. This consolidation leads to the loss of competition within the medical industry and higher costs.

We have been moving toward an oligopoly in the healthcare industry with Medicare and a handful of major medical insurance providers dealing with a handful of healthcare providers and a handful of drug companies. With this oligopoly, is it any wonder medical costs have gone through the roof? Bigger is not better.

MEDICARE BROKE

Is Medicare running out of money and if so why and what can we do about it?

The Medicare umbrella includes retirement benefits, disability benefits, and low income Medicaid with a complex arrangement of plans A, B, C, D, supplements, and state participation in Medicaid. The plan, which covers 49 million people, began in 1966. Prior to that, people without company plans paid their own medical bills or did without. Since then and particularly over the past few decades, medical costs have risen faster than overall inflation, the economy, and faster than payroll taxes (see earlier healthcare discussions for an explanation). Thus, Medicare has become severely underfunded. If it were a corporate plan, it would be at risk of bankrupting the business.

How did we get into this mess?

People are living longer and requiring medical care over longer periods. Life expectancy at age 65 has risen from 15.3 years to 17.5 years since the 1960s. In addition, mortality prior to age 65 has declined so that the percentage of those who reach age 21 and go on to reach age 65 has climbed from 65.7% to 78.0% since the 1960s. This is important because the number of workers who pay into the plan and don't reach age 65 has declined. Yet the retirement age to receive Medicare hasn't changed.

At the same time, as noted earlier, healthcare costs have exploded since the 1960s and payroll taxes to pay for this increase have not kept pace. Part of the problem is that the plan wasn't set up to be self-funded. The maximum that people put into the plan (including employer match) is about $120,000 over their working lifetime, and most people pay much less. Yet the average healthcare cost over that person's retirement averages $200,000 or more.

In the 1960s when the plan was put into effect, the sponsors counted on the large number of Baby-boomers supporting their parents in retirement. Since then, people have been having smaller families and the worker/retiree ratio no longer works.

Yet the government has failed to address the issue.

OPTIONS TO FIX MEDICARE

What can we do about the Medicare mess we've inherited due to political miscalculations and reluctance to take this on, going all the way back to the 1960s?

1. **Continue to do nothing**. It has been a popular path for our leaders to kick the can down the road for the next generation to deal with. Doing nothing means continuing to rob funds from the Social Security retirement plan. It also means that any solution taken later will be even more painful than if taken now.
2. **Increase payroll tax rates**. If we just increase the rate, we will need to double the current 1.45% employee payroll tax rate to 3.2% to cover current spending and higher to fully fund the retiree medical costs of current employees. Such a tax increase will be unpopular with most workers.
3. **Continue to cover the Medicare spending shortfall from general tax revenues**. The problem with this is Medicare already costs over half a trillion dollars per year (that's with a big "T"). If costs aren't dealt with, the tax burden will drag down the U.S. economy, which means less jobs and lower pay for American workers.
4. **For high income individuals, increase taxes and increase premiums**. Already, high income individuals pay higher payroll taxes than lower income people for the identical same Medicare benefits. In addition, they also pay significantly higher premiums for Medicare B and for the

drug coverage (Medicare D). They also pay higher income taxes to cover the Medicare spending shortfall. How much more still fits within the definition of "fair?"

5. **Privatize**. This is a very controversial idea. Given how out of control medical costs have been for decades in the private sector as well as with Medicare, this is a speculative solution without much evidence it will help. The core problems with sky-high medical costs are:
   - Consolidation of payers to a handful of insurance companies and Medicare, who pass along cost increases in premiums and general tax revenues. Moving control from Medicare to huge insurance carriers will not improve this.
   - Industry consolidation, which eliminates competition among healthcare providers.
   - The fact that with insurance, consumers often only have to pay 20% or less of the cost, which encourages higher prices and more procedures.
6. **Reduce drug company costs**. This talk centers around having Medicare use its muscle to negotiate with the drug companies. Short of using coercion, will this really bring down the costs enough to make a difference? After all, drug companies are expert at gaming the system. They jack up prices as the basis to begin negotiations. Only a free market can bring down prices and that doesn't work in the oligopoly that we are rapidly approaching.
7. **Allow Americans to import drugs from overseas**. Having Medicare cover those costs will require additional measures to ensure the quality of the overseas drugs coming from countries that don't have U.S. drug standards. There have been cases of bad drugs reaching the United States with impurities or otherwise failing to meet FDA quality.
8. **Launch a Moon-landing type challenge to find treatments and cures for Alzheimer's, diabetes, heart disease, and cancer**. These four diseases account for some three-quarters of Medicare costs. This offers the opportunity to improve lives as well as to reduce costs over time. For that reason alone, this would be a worthy endeavor. However, if these diseases are greatly reduced

Then again, for millions of Americans who didn't have medical coverage before, expansion of the private insurance market place provided a safety net against catastrophic medical costs. Unfortunately, several of the state marketplaces have failed, leaving many Americans with no coverage again.

Those who want to repeal ACA object to it on several grounds, including that this legislation was guided by big drug companies, insurance companies, and others who stand to benefit by being able to consolidate, squeeze out competition, and gain more participants mandated by the Federal government with penalties to those who don't purchase insurance. It was a big win for drug and health insurance companies.

However, ACA-rejecters haven't come up with a better alternative healthcare delivery system that addresses the escalating healthcare costs seen during the decades before ACA with availability to every American who wants insurance. The only suggestion from this group seems to be less regulation, but the industry has already consolidated and healthcare costs have already grown to 17.5% of the economy.

What would cause the ACA to fail would be to remove the controversial mandatory feature with penalties. If that happens, healthy people will opt out of the expensive insurance marketplaces, causing premiums to escalate even further.

Returning to the old healthcare system is not the answer.

HEALTHCARE TRANSPARENCY

How can we deal with out-of-control healthcare costs?

First, how many of us get irritated when we buy a car? We negotiate a price. Then we go to close the deal and get all the add-ons they try to sell us: security etching, extended warranties, and more. That's tame by comparison to the healthcare industry.

Pharmacies often won't tell us how much a prescription will cost until we're ready to pay. They claim they can't know until they submit the bill to insurance. That's a cop-out in the digital age.

On the other hand, do you really care how much insurance pays on your behalf? After all, it's not coming out of your pocket. You should. In one way or another we're paying for the insurance costs either through premiums, taxes or a weaker job market.

When you go in for an MRI or other procedure, and if you're willing to pay cash and not use insurance, they may quote you a cash price in advance. They benefit by not having to file forms, wait for insurance companies to wade through the claims, and then take whatever insurance companies deem as normal and customary.

If you plan to use insurance, it can be tough to get the facility to give you a quote. They'll say they have to submit the claim and see what insurance pays. They will happily bill you the rest. I shopped around for MRI costs a while back and was quoted numbers (before insurance) ranging from $500 to $10,000 for the same procedure. When I asked why, the high-priced provider said that's how the game is played.

The game!

It's a racket and shifting the cost to general taxes or the "rich" won't make that problem go away. That will make it worse unless we face the issue of out-of-control costs head on.

If you need a medical procedure, you take your chances. The surgeon will have his or her fee, then there's the anesthesiologist, the facility cost, and a long list of other providers and supplies. Even worse is a hospital stay. None of these people will venture a guess as to what it will cost you. They've gotten used to people taking their services no matter what it costs and leaving the matter up to their insurance company. As a result, the prices keep going up.

A positive suggestion would be to require that every healthcare provider publish its costs, prices, and results beforehand so people know what they're buying. Give people the option of comparison shopping. Give us transparency.

HEALTHCARE OPTIONS

Okay, what options do we have to deal with healthcare costs that have already reached 17.5% of our economy?

Every couple of years, candidates come around talking about how we should tackle healthcare. In the past, many people have tried and failed.

1. Managed care was hot in the 1990s. It provided lower patient costs in exchange for limiting the selection of healthcare providers to those who would allow the insurance company to control costs. In essence, the healthcare providers worked as employees rather than charging fees for service. The limited selection did not win over enough patients to make this work. Most people want to be able to choose their own doctors.
2. Insurance companies have promoted in/out of network to control costs as well as generic vs. brand drugs. These have softened the impact of healthcare inflation, though only until patients and healthcare providers made this one-time adjustment. Then costs continued to climb, reflecting the inherent lack of incentives to control costs.
3. A recent development has been the introduction of high-deductible plans with tax-favored savings accounts (Medical Savings Accounts (1996) and Health Savings Accounts (2003)). The idea is that patients would be self-insured up to a limit, typically around $2500 per person. By being self-insured, patients would take more ownership of

> their routine medical needs. The hope is that patients will have the incentive to question costs and unnecessary procedures. The reality is quite different. Only about 5% of covered workers are in high-deductible plans. Most people don't want to have to deal with the possibility that as a family they might have to pay the first $5,000 (two-person limit) of costs. They would rather pay higher premiums for a lower deductible plan. For corporate plans, employees often only pay 20% of the insurance premiums. That makes it hard for companies to offer enough incentives to get employees to take this risk. In any case, it's impossible for 5% of patients to have any impact on negotiating overall healthcare costs.

One proposal to get patients to pay closer attention to the cost of healthcare and thus to push back on rising costs would be to make the employee healthcare benefit taxable. It is estimated that employees receive some $133 billion in untaxed healthcare benefits, making it one of the largest tax loopholes. If this became taxed and tax rates were reduced to offset this change to make the change revenue neutral, employees would see how much their healthcare costs are going up.

Yet in the past, when companies provided this information, employees had no idea what to do with it. So what if my company paid $X in medical premiums on my behalf? What can I do about it? After all, companies negotiate with the insurance carriers who negotiate with the providers. The costs are a pooling from thousands of patients.

Information is only useful if it helps to change behavior. This won't, and making individual employees pay taxes on their medical premiums won't give them the tools to push back on the costs. In fact it might encourage more people to drop medical insurance.

Another suggestion might be to segment healthcare in the following way. Maybe it makes sense from a national health and security standpoint to have a national healthcare plan that covers communicable diseases that can be administered through current healthcare providers. It would be in our national interest that all communicable diseases be dealt with in the quickest manner possible. The recent Ebola crisis should be a wakeup call.

Under this proposal, every contagious disease that could

become a national epidemic, including HIV, would be covered by this plan. This would also cover vaccinations against communicable diseases, and provide a national focus for dealing with the Zika virus.

Some people might argue that this is a first step toward a single-payer system, and maybe to some it is. Yet, these illnesses should be a national security concern. It's not in our best interests as a nation for people to avoid healthcare for diseases when they can't pay. That only makes an epidemic worse.

If we want to address the continued increase in healthcare costs, here are some options:

1. Open up healthcare insurance across state lines. This would allow people who move not to have to reapply for insurance, often at higher rates. It would also increase competition among insurance carriers, which should help bring down costs.
2. Deal with what is becoming too-big-to-fail in the healthcare industry. We have a shrinking number of major insurance companies that are getting bigger and more concentrated with each passing decade. Perhaps it's time to apply Teddy Roosevelt's antitrust standards to healthcare before it is too late. That would also apply to the consolidation in the pharmacy industry.
3. Require transparency on costs and medical results from healthcare providers so that patients have the information to make decisions.
4. Provide a standardized two-tier premium system in which the lower tier would be for those without pre-existing conditions and the higher would be for those with pre-existing conditions at a premium no more than 20% above the base premium. Make it a requirement that companies cannot reject anyone from tier 2. This would remove the hiked up premiums to healthier participants while still providing guaranteed insurance to those with pre-existing conditions at a somewhat higher rate.
5. Provide incentives to promote high-deductible healthcare plans that put the patient back in the driver's seat relative to costs and incentives to push back, up to a limit. This would turn insurance into a catastrophic medical plan. Perhaps we would want to waive the deductible for

> communicable diseases and certain well-patient visits. If such plans were to become a third of all plans or more, patients would have more incentive to push back and shop around for medical costs. Now, it is true that we have little control over emergencies, but we do have control over selection of pharmacies, which often have different prices, and on brand vs. generic and various generic alternatives.

In other words, put patients back in control of choosing healthcare providers and drug alternatives. Provide them the transparency and tools to negotiate costs and make decisions. Obviously emergency situations are not conducive to patient cost control, but many other healthcare needs are.

There may be other ways to handle emergency room injuries and life-threatening diseases that don't escalate the overall cost of healthcare if we can get beyond our attachment or aversion to ACA. In any case, we can't just assume we've dealt with affordability by shifting the escalating costs of healthcare to "wealthy" people. This would further remove the decision to spend on healthcare from those who have to pay, locking in the cycle of escalating costs.

In the end, the cost of healthcare will be borne by all Americans as it drags down the U.S. economy.

SINGLE PAYER HEALTHCARE PITCH

Would a single-payer healthcare system cure America's healthcare problems?

Many people believe so. Some candidates look at the failure of ACA to cover all Americans and seek to replace it with an expanded Medicare for all Americans. What's not to like about a single-payer system for the United States?

A. One appeal is simplicity. We get to replace our company provided healthcare plans (78% of working Americans are covered by company plans) with Medicare, which comes in flavors of Plans A, B, C, and D, along with the need to select a medical supplement insurance. The supplement comes in flavors of A, B, C, F, F high deductible, G, K, L, and N. Then, annually you need to select the drug coverage for Plan D. With the exception of Plan A, they all come with individual premiums for each participant, which go up annually for the participant's age as well as for the inflationary cost of escalating healthcare. Perhaps it's not as simple for those with company plans that often pay 80% of the premium costs.

B. A second appeal is that it would cover everyone or at least everyone who paid their Plan B, C, D, and supplement premiums. Those premiums, which can be controlled by Congress, are lower than private insurance available through ACA. This will encourage more Americans to pay in to get their coverage. However, Medicare premiums are lower than private insurance because they are subsidized by payroll taxes and by general tax revenues. Increasing the number of beneficiaries to include all Americans will significantly increase the government subsidies that will have to come from tax increases. After all, Medicare is already not a self-funding plan.

C. A third appeal is potentially lower healthcare premiums for most Americans. A prevailing plan has employers paying the majority of the additional payroll taxes to cover universal Medicare. Remember that Medicare is not a self-funded plan, meaning it draws on general tax revenues to meet its obligations. That means higher income taxes will be required. In addition, workers currently have to pay in for a number of years to qualify for Medicare. Perhaps that will be waived in the new plan so the plan can cover everyone. The government could expand its subsidized premiums such that lower income individuals would pay lower premiums for Plans B, C, and D based on annual income, meaning that someone else has to pay more. For the 78% of Americans covered by company medical plans, they pay something like 20% of the company's medical insurance premiums today and thus for them, their costs will go up. It's not clear how employees covered by company plans will be saving thousands of dollars a year with the new plan. For those who pay their full premiums, their premiums should go down since Medicare premiums are subsidized. That means someone else has to pay taxes to cover the subsidy.

D. A fourth appeal is the promise that the administrative costs of healthcare would be lower than the current system that uses health insurance companies. With Medicare covering all except the Medicare Supplement Insurance, there would be less private insurance administrative costs and profits in the system. There could also be a consolidation of Medicaid and VA plans into a single plan. That promises to save administrative costs. This streamlining in theory should reduce overall costs. That assumes that the U.S. government can efficiently manage the largest medical system in the world, representing

17.5% of the economy with a single agency.

E. A fifth appeal of using Medicare as a single-payer system for all Americans is the promised emphasis on negotiating cost reductions. Here it gets tricky. The pitch is that the expanded government program would be in a position to negotiate large medical cost savings from drug companies, doctors, and hospitals. The reality is that when people are faced with lower income, they tend to make different decisions. After a one-time adjustment to the new plan, drug companies, doctors, and hospitals will either adapt or go out of business, reducing the supply of healthcare providers to service a larger group of patients now that everyone is covered.

Already there are doctors and facilities that do not take Medicare. Will more leave if Medicare becomes the nationwide single provider and pushes down payments? If Medicare rolls back medical costs to say the 1990s levels to bring spending under control, it could lead to a shortage of doctors and longer patient waiting, especially for non-emergency procedures.

The drug world is even more complicated. It appears that drug research and development in the United States is strong for popular medicines with the incentive being the high prices and profits to be had through sales in the United States. Certain third world countries do not respect American patent law and make knock-off drugs, which are shipped around the world at much lower prices than in the United States. The drug companies fight this yet tolerate the condition since they get to recover their research and FDA approval costs through sales in the United States.

Americans are subsidizing this research for the world. Single-payer systems in other countries rely to some extent on this American subsidy of research costs to make their plans work. To push for the same prices in the United States would correct this unfairness but would create another side-effect. With no way to recover the costs of research and FDA approval, the drug companies will have less incentives to develop new drugs at a time when antibiotic resistant bacteria have made many of our current medicines obsolete.

The single-payer plan relies on doctors, hospitals, and drug companies taking less money while providing more services to cover the increased number of Americans covered. Good luck with that.

SINGLE PAYER SIDE-EFFECTS

What side-effects would expanding Medicare into a national single-payer system bring with it?

1. A nationwide single-payer Medicare plan will decimate the health insurance industry while increasing the Federal Medicare bureaucracy. During this process, most of the 492,000 healthcare insurance employees will lose their jobs. That will ripple through the economy.
2. It will be necessary to significantly raise taxes to cover the costs of subsidizing hundreds of millions of new participants in Medicare. Remember that Medicare is not a self-funded plan. Some candidates promise that this tax increase will come from the "rich." More on the effects of increasing taxes later.
3. Expanding Medicare to all Americans will expand the size and role of the government. It will promote continued consolidation within the healthcare industry. We will end up with fewer and bigger drug companies and fewer and larger hospital/doctor conglomerates as they struggle to deal with increased government regulation and scrutiny.
4. A single U.S. payer along with the surviving drug company oligopoly and only a few hospital/doctor networks will administer medicine on a political basis instead of on a patient basis. Anyone who believes this is a great idea hasn't listened to the problems within the veteran's administration healthcare system.

5. Even with all the bravado about big government negotiating better costs from doctors, hospitals, and drug companies, this plan doesn't address a fundamental reality of rising medical costs. Since patients won't be paying for their own healthcare because the plan shifts the burden of payment to taxes on the top 1-3%, no one has a direct incentive to hold costs down. Patients will pass their costs to Medicare. The government simply passes costs onto taxpayers. The top 1-3% group is not in a position to negotiate medical prices. Besides, providers will come up with creative ways to meet their revenue/income needs through additional procedures and when your health is at stake, who is to say what isn't necessary?
6. Without a free and open market, the government will lose its measure of what is an appropriate cost for services other than political expediency. Right now, insurance companies and Medicare look at "normal and customary" fees around the country as a yardstick. Once big government brings a consolidation within the drug, hospital, and doctor groups, there will no longer be independent "normal and customary" fees to compare to.
7. Finally, single-payer systems like Canada tend to do better than the current American healthcare system for critical care services, while not doing as well for non-critical care services, such as hip replacements, where patients face long delays.

The point is that any solution to the healthcare system will bring along significant side-effects and disruption, and few proposals deal with the underlying problem, which is increasing costs.

Now, if you're an advocate of a single-payer system, you might say stop throwing cold water on our amazing plans. Don't be so negative, always looking at the downside. Well, I hear skydiving can be quite exciting and perhaps you don't want some gloomy guy pointing out that you don't have a parachute, but jumping without it can be exhilarating until the end.

The bottom line is that any solution to the healthcare crisis will be painful and the best solution is to push forward with full disclosure to the American people.

PART 4: WAGES

≈≈≈≈≈≈≈≈≈≈≈≈≈≈≈≈≈

INCOME INEQUALITY

Much has been said about the concentration of wealth over the past decades in the hands of the billionaires, as well as income inequality.

But wealth is not income.

Whereas one family controls more wealth than the bottom 130 million Americans, when it comes to income, the top 0.001% (the top 1,400 households) making over $45 million a year have only 1.9% of the nation's income according to the IRS. That's significant, though not as skewed as certain candidates would have you believe.

Candidates give us the mantra that "trillions of dollars have gone from middle and lower class families to the wealthy." That simply isn't true. It might feel true, but here are the facts. Over the past few decades, middle and lower class compensation has barely kept up with inflation. That is true. If their real incomes (after inflation) had gone down, then we could argue that they gave up income to the rich. But that hasn't happened. The most we can honestly say is that the top 0.001% (1,400 households) got theirs and didn't share.

As noted earlier, if the billionaires redistributed their billions to all Americans, it would only amount to a one-time $6,250 payment per person. That would not cover the grief that middle and lower income families are facing. That is the inconvenient truth of campaign promises about the redistribution of wealth. Sure we'd all like to receive that $6,250 check, but then what? It won't increase our wages or solve any of a myriad other problems, though it might make us feel better for a brief time.

We are told that Americans are working longer hours for lower wages. In fact, overall real compensation (after inflation) was flat over the past couple of decades, not lower. Certainly there are many individuals who are worse off, which needs to be addressed by getting the economy to grow more jobs.

While household income for middle and low income families has been flat, household size has declined by 4% since 1995, by 17% since 1972, before the malaise of the 1970s, and 24% since 1960. Thus, over the past 50 years, household size has shrunk and there are more two income families supporting smaller families.

We are told that income inequality is due to lower taxes for the wealthy. Yet, the 2002-03 tax cut that gets blamed for the recent income/wealth inequality only amounted to a 7.6% increase in after-tax income to those affected. Besides, very little of the billionaire wealth gets taxed each year. It's not enough to account for the growing inequality.

On the other hand, Federal Reserve (Fed) policy has been cited as a cause, particularly in the years after 9/11, when they have tried to keep the economy from descending into a depression. After that attack, the Fed boosted the money supply to deal with the economic uncertainty that followed. Federal mortgage companies were encouraged to boost loans to keep the economy going. The resulting bubble in real estate and stocks benefitted the top 0.01% far more than the small reduction in taxes. At the same time, the middle class who depended on interest income got hurt by the lower interest rates.

Perhaps we should pay closer attention to Fed policy rather than tax rates as the cause of income and wealth inequality.

At the same time, the American economy is continuing its transformation to more information based technologies while our educational system struggles to adapt and keep up. Workers would benefit from improving the quality of education so that companies aren't looking to immigrants and outsourcing to find the talent they need.

The income gap between the top 1% and the middle/lower classes has been reported to be the highest since the 1920s. The raw numbers do show that 5 of the top 15 gap years were during 2005-12 and 9 were 1913-29. Statistically this is correct, though it ignores payments like Social Security, refundable tax credits, and various welfare programs available today. Those programs are not included in this calculation and were not available during 1913-29. Including those non-income payments would reduce the recent income gap.

We also shouldn't forget that even the poor today are much better off than the middle class of the 1920s with far more conveniences. As an example, today we spend far less on food than in the 1920s. In other words, every group has seen improvements. Yet we feel disappointed and betrayed because our expectations aren't being met and many people feel trapped, unable to climb the ladder of success.

The level of wealth inequality is concerning relative to our democratic values. There is a sense in a democracy that we should all start out equal and yet inherited wealth gives some people advantages not available to others.

There are two ways to address this. One is the mantra blaming the billionaires and the rich for whatever ails us and try to pull them down. That will create for them a new set of incentives to avoid taxes rather than investing in products and services that create more jobs.

The second path would be to raise up the poor with better jobs. That will require better education and an economic environment that stops squeezing small businesses that have been the engine of growth. It will also require managing the economy with incentives to continue to grow and create new jobs. Part of that managing would require balancing the supply of labor by examining the amount of immigration until wages reach a more equitable level.

PART 4: WAGES

≈≈≈≈≈≈≈≈≈≈≈≈≈≈≈≈≈

OUTSOURCING

Aside from blaming the rich, the primary mantra for why wages have been depressed for decades has been the outsourcing of jobs to China and Mexico. What was the full effect of this outsourcing?

Outsourcing began in the 1980s and accelerated in the 1990s as a result of two key decisions. First was the decision by many companies to turn over their production to contract manufacturers, whose focus was on producing products and on the logistics of moving products around. The lure was that a contract manufacturer that focused on manufacturing could operate more efficiently than dozens of companies torn between new product development, marketing, and manufacturing. This trend took off in the late 1990s during the technology bubble.

Outsourcing to American contract manufacturers allowed the originating companies to focus on products and markets and to use the contract manufacturers to scale up manufacturing at a much more rapid pace than they could do themselves. This was particularly helpful to new startup operations.

Then, under pressure to reduce manufacturing costs, these contract manufacturers moved their production to Mexico and to China.

Second, big box stores traditionally were proud to buy made-in-America. In the late 1990s, as they fought to reduce costs and prices in order to compete, they changed direction. By forcing their suppliers to accept prices they couldn't meet in America, they pushed hundreds of manufacturers to outsource in order to survive. The decision for these suppliers was to source overseas or to go out of business. Thus began the flood of jobs to China and Mexico. When you buy from big-box stores today, you're buying from the engine that pushed jobs overseas.

As the mad dash to outsource jobs grew after 2000, companies moved their own manufacturing operations to China. Often they failed to fully analyze the cost of shipping, the longer lead times, and communications issues resulting from language and cultural differences. The mantra became: To avoid high U.S. labor costs it has to be cheaper overseas. It was another mantra without the facts to support it.

Having analyzed some of these decisions after the fact, I discovered that these moves turned out disastrous for companies who lost control of their products, their quality, and in some cases, their businesses to Chinese companies.

In one case, a U.S. manufacturer, convinced that China was cheaper, transferred production to a Chinese company. That Chinese company produced for its U.S. sponsor on the day shift and then went into competition with subsidized costs on their night shift. That destroyed the market for the U.S. business. It wasn't alone.

This outsourcing trend accelerated during the past 15 years. Between 2001 and 2013, some 3.2 million jobs moved to China and another 700,000 moved to Mexico. If you were one of those, my heart goes out to you. I hope you've found something else.

While this was hard for those who lost jobs, let's look at the overall manufacturing sector during this time period.

According to the St. Louis Federal Reserve Bank (Fed), there were 17.3 million manufacturing jobs in 2000 and 12.3 million in 2015, for an overall loss of 5.0 million. Using the average annual productivity rate during this time of 3.5%, we would have expected 40% fewer jobs needed to produce the same output in 2015 as in 2000 or 7.0 million fewer jobs (40% of 17.3 million). Over that time period, the economy grew 30%. Assuming manufacturing held its share of the jobs remaining after productivity gains, 3.1 million (30% of (17.3-7.0)) manufacturing jobs should have been created due to economic growth.

Thus, 2015 manufacturing jobs should have been 13.4 million

(see chart below) based on productivity and overall economic growth. Actual jobs were therefore 1.1 million less than expected (12.3 vs. 13.4), and this assumes that manufacturing would have grown at the same rate as healthcare and other services, which we know it hasn't because healthcare is growing faster than the rest of the economy.

	Manufacturing Jobs (millions)
Manufacturing jobs 2000	17.3
Expected loss (productivity)	(7.0)
GDP growth 30%	3.1
Calculated jobs	13.4
Actual jobs	12.3
Missing jobs	1.1

Therefore, while we did lose 3.2 million jobs to China and 700,000 jobs to Mexico, we are only 1.1 million jobs below where we would have been without the outsourcing. What this means is if all those jobs return to the United States, they won't look like the jobs that left.

How can this be?

If you're one of those who lost your job, this makes no sense. Yet, this isn't the first time an entire sector of the economy has shrunk. In 1900, 38% of Americans lived on farms. In the 19th century it was over 70%. Now it is 1-2%. This occurred because of farm productivity. With only 1-2% of the workforce, we produce enough food to export. If we had preserved all of the farm jobs from 1900, we would not have achieved the economic growth over the past 115 years that brought cars, cell phones, and other products and services we've come to depend on.

Yet that's no comfort to those who have lost their jobs.

Throughout corporate America, executives have made decisions relative to outsourcing jobs to China and Mexico despite the logistical and coordination complexities associated with doing this. Companies don't want to have to deal with the logistics and coordination problems. Yet, many companies have moved due to labor cost differences and regulations.

Among workers affected by these decisions, there is a belief that companies have sold out this country for a few extra points of margin so they can compete. Is this necessary?

One of the positive side-effects of outsourcing to China and Mexico has been lower prices that have benefited millions of middle class and poor Americans. It has also led to lower wages as it dried up a large number of jobs, thus putting downward pressure on wages.

One path to resolve this problem would be to look at contract manufacturing and big-box store practices to determine how to bring the best jobs back to America. Some manufacturers are already realizing the mistake of having to deal with transportation and delivery issues of getting products from China and Mexico. As China's wages push up, more companies will be forced to reexamine their decisions.

Probably the most immediate and significant action the United States could take to curb outsourcing would be to join our trading partners with a Value Added Tax (VAT) offset by lower corporate income tax rates and less tax loopholes. Together, these would make manufacturing in the United States more competitive without stirring a trade war, since our trading partners already are using VAT to encourage their exports.

Isn't it time we leveled the playing field? At the same time, we need to address the escalating healthcare costs that make manufacturing in the United States uncompetitive.

DEPRESSED WAGES

Various candidates have said that real wages have been flat over some 15, 30, or 50 years or so. Everyone is pointing fingers, often at the billionaires, at outsourcing, and at trade. What are the facts?

Between 1979 and 2013, productivity grew 64.9%, while real hourly compensation for production and nonsupervisory workers grew just 8.2%. Productivity thus grew eight times faster than typical hourly compensation. From 1973-1991, real hourly compensation dropped in 13 out of 18 years, losing 4.8% over the 18 years. From 1991-2013 (22 years), real compensation rose during 16 of those years for a total increase of 14.9%, though much less than productivity increases. Hourly compensation was lower in 2013 than it was in 2009 and 2010.

Thus, it's true that real hourly compensation lost ground from 1973 through 1991. It gained from 1991 to 2013, though much less than productivity. The important question is why.

The inconvenient truth is "supply and demand." In its simplest form, imagine you wanted to sell a used car (supply). You find three interested people (demand). As they compete to buy your car, you can expect a higher price than if there were three people selling similar cars (supply) and only one person is interested.

When demand goes up, so does the price. Recall what happened to housing prices between 2002 and 2007 when banks made easy mortgages. People bought expensive homes they couldn't otherwise afford. Then again, when supply is higher than demand, which happened to housing after the crash, prices plunged. The same thing has happened to hourly compensation.

Before you say, "No, no, that's propaganda," imagine that you live in a small town with one burger shop that employs six people. You decide to get a summer job. You go down and plead with the owner. There are only six jobs and now seven people who want them. Unemployment now includes you and you need the job.

The owner fires someone who has been late almost every day over the past month and hires you at a lower wage since you don't have the experience. Because the fired person is looking for a new job, unemployment remains higher than before you started looking for a job. Average wages are down since the owner is paying you less than the guy he fired.

The fired individual walks down the street and pleads with the hardware store owner to give him a job at less than he was making at the burger shop, because he needs the job. This action cascades across the town, driving down wages until the grocery store decides it can afford to add a new job at the lower wage. At that point, unemployment goes back down, but the average wage in town is lower than before you decided to get into the job market.

The quickest way to drive down hourly compensation is to have more people looking for jobs than there are jobs available. We all know this if we have ever had to line up with dozens or more other people trying to fill a single job.

You're thinking: Outsourcing reduced available jobs. You would be correct to the tune of 4 million jobs, but another factor has been at play over the past 60 years.

My mother was a single mom struggling to get by on what she could earn by teaching. She and many other women needed jobs either to support themselves or to help their families. Women entered the workforce in large numbers during World War II when men entered military service for the war. After the war, many of these women lost their jobs as the men returned, but they'd had a taste of working for pay.

As far as hourly compensation is concerned, despite all of the positive aspects and contributions of more women participating in the workforce, the increased participation represented an additional supply of labor, which acted to push down average wages. One of the inconvenient truths of more inclusion in the workplace as seen in the chart below is that increases in participation have depressed hourly compensation.

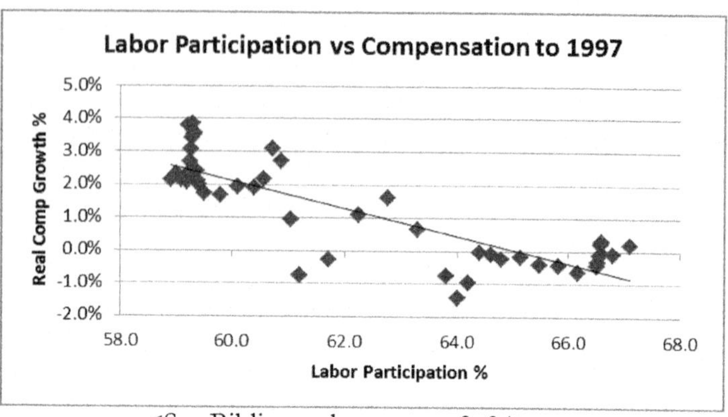

<See Bibliography sources 3, 34>

The overall participation rate was unchanged between 1948 and 1965. While the female (age 25-54) participation went up from 35% to over 45%, participation by people under 25 and over 55 declined. From 1966 to 1997, the overall participation went up from 59% to 67%, adding an average of 0.4% additional workers each year. During this time period, female participation (age 25-54) increased from 45% to 77%, after which, it leveled out.

With no increase in the overall labor participation until 1966, despite the increase in women, there was no downward pressure on compensation. When the participation rate did take off in 1966 through 1973, the economy was growing at 4.0% and thus absorbed the additional workers without depressing compensation. Real compensation grew a total of 18% or 2.1% per year during this time.

Years	Average Real Compensation Change	Change in Labor Participation M/F 16 & over	Real GDP
1952-65	2.9%	0.0%	3.8%
1966-73	2.1%	0.4%	4.0%
1974-82	-0.2%	0.6%	2.1%
1983-97	-0.1%	0.3%	3.6%
1998-13	0.8%	0.0%	2.2%

From 1974 through 1982, the economy only grew 2.1% per year, while the participation rate was growing at 0.6% per year, the highest rate over the entire time period. The female (age 25-54) and the overall participation rates both reached 64%. Compensation fell between 1974 and 1982 by an average 0.2% per year, the worst time period.

Then, from 1983-97, the economy grew an average 3.6% while the participation rate slowed to 0.3% per year, reaching 67% in 1997. During this time, the female participation grew to 77%. Meanwhile, male (age 25-54) participation dropped to 92% in 1997 and to 90.5% by 2005, and participation for black males dropped to 83%. The difference in female participation between 1948 and 2005 means that 29 million more women are working today than would have under 1948's participation rate. Compare that to 4 million jobs lost due to outsourcing.

Despite the 3.6% economic growth and slower increase in participation, real compensation declined from 1983 through 1997. After 1997, the participation rate leveled off, removing the downward pressure on compensation.

What else is going on here?

Prior to the 1965 Immigration and Nationality Act, the pace of immigration had been low, which may have contributed to the rise in real hourly compensation through the 1950s and 1960s. Then, over the past 50 years, the United States absorbed 43 million net new immigrants and 11.2 million illegal immigrants. The economy has done a marvelous job of absorbing these additional workers without collapsing wages altogether. Sadly, compensation has not kept pace with productivity.

An inconvenient truth of immigration is that when we have faster rates of immigration we also have lower compensation growth (see chart below). The best compensation growth has been when 5-year immigration has been below 1%, or 0.2% per year. Immigration has been above that rate since 1988, after the last illegal immigrant amnesty.

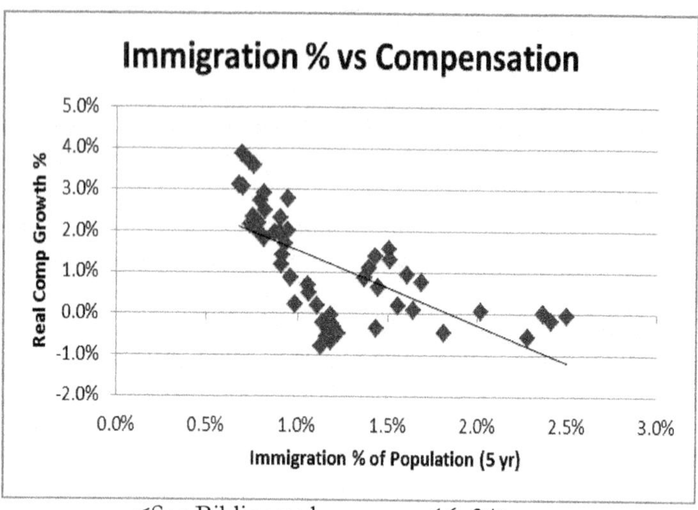

<See Bibliography sources 16, 34>

Combining the change in labor participation and immigration as a percentage of the population and comparing to real compensation shows an even stronger correlation. As more people enter the workforce from labor participation and immigration, real compensation growth drops. When less people enter the workforce, compensation growth is higher.

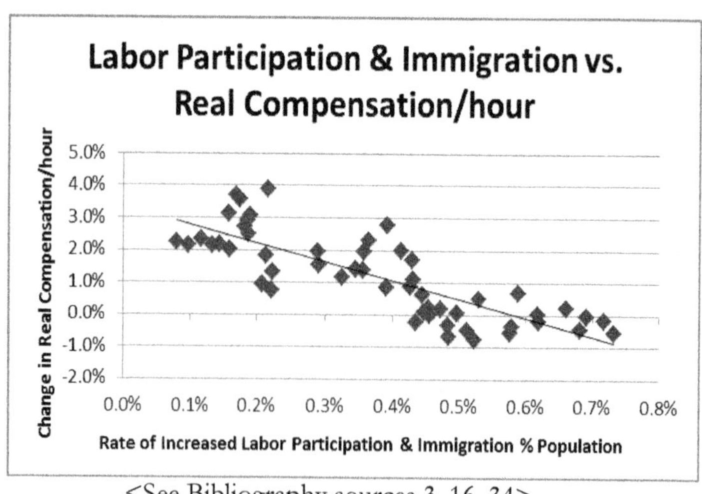

<See Bibliography sources 3, 16, 34>

The highest real compensation growth (2.7%) occurred from 1949-1972 while the combined growth in labor participation and immigration represented only 0.2% of the population per year. Real compensation was flat from 1976-1997 during which the combined growth in labor participation and immigration represented 0.6% of the population.

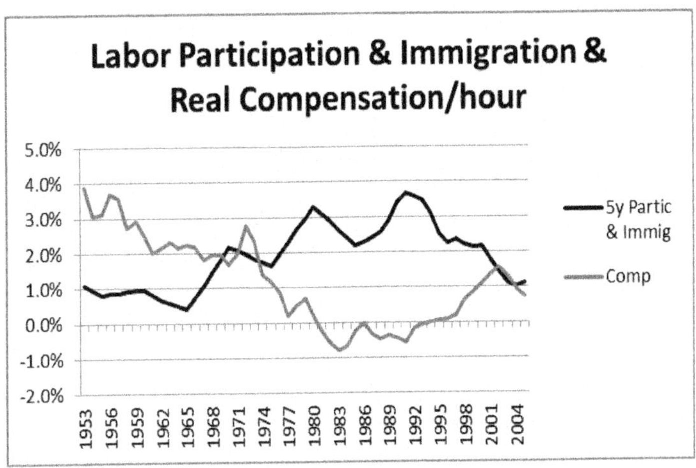

The difference between 0.2% and 0.6% is 1.25 million people. From 1998-2013, real compensation/hour increased 0.8% per year while the combined growth in labor participation and immigration represented 0.3% of the population.

People will point to the 3.2 million jobs that have been outsourced to China as the cause of stagnant wages and that has certainly contributed over the past 15 years. They will argue that companies will always try to push down wages. That is true. They ignore the fact that unions and workers will always try to push up wages either in the private sector or through the political process.

What balances the push by companies to lower wages and by employees to increase wages is the supply of jobs and of workers. When the supply of workers goes up, the companies win this tug of war. They win due to outsourcing, but also due to labor participation and immigration.

Relative to the outsourcing argument, compensation began to stagnate in the early 1970s long before trade with China took off and in fact had its worst time period before outsourcing became so big. Besides, those 4 million outsourced jobs are dwarfed by the 29 million additional women who entered the workforce and the workers associated with additional immigration and illegal immigration.

The downsides of illegal immigration have been two fold. First has been the increased supply of labor chasing jobs. Second has been the willingness of these workers to work at much less than citizens, thus depressing wages of Americans and legal immigrants.

The question we might ask is how has the economy absorbed so many additional workers without real compensation going down and what can we learn from this.

The population increase spurred by immigration has increased the demand for goods and services, which has increased the need for workers. More women with jobs have increased the demand for goods and services, though the increase in demand has not been enough to drive up compensation. We also have had a weak economic recovery after 2009 that has not created as many jobs as in prior recoveries.

Comparing today to the booming 1990s might tickle nostalgia, but through rose-colored glasses. The 1990s boom was driven in part by the stock market bubble that burst in 2000. Day trading took off, creating instant millionaires and when it crashed, instant paupers. Even the head of the Federal Reserve warned about "irrational exuberance" in the months leading up to the crash.

While high immigration and the increase in labor participation have been associated with depressed wages, women and immigrants are not to blame. They were only trying to improve their lives.

Race and gender have nothing to do with depressed wages. Simply put, when more workers enter the labor force either through participation or immigration, it pushes wages down to absorb them until the economy can adjust. Compensation began to lag in 1973 when labor force participation went up and continued through the high immigration over the past 25 years.

The lessons from history are clear. When the economy is rapidly growing as it was during the 1960's, it can better absorb participation increases and immigrants. When the economy is slower as it has been over the past 15 years, then more immigration leads to slower compensation growth.

In summary, the causes of depressed wages have been 1) the increased participation rate, 2) increased immigration, 3) outsourcing, and 4) healthcare costs. We can chant mantras about the billionaires, greedy companies, and outsourcing, but unless we focus on the real issues, we are not going to break out of this cycle.

The female and total labor participation rates have been flat since the mid-1990s, so that hasn't been a factor since then. Legal immigration remains higher than during the time period of higher real compensation growth. Including illegal immigration puts the recent pace of immigration at the highest since the 1920s.

If we can manage the immigrant flow and deal with illegal immigration to allow something like 500,000 total immigrants per year, we should be able to see compensation levels increase over the next decade. At the same time, we can encourage businesses to bring jobs back by adopting a Value Added Tax that will level the international trade playing field. The retiring of the Baby Boom generation could also reduce the supply of labor, which would push up wage rates. Finally, we need to address out of control healthcare costs or that burden will continue to make American jobs uncompetitive.

MINIMUM WAGE

Increasing the minimum wage is the quickest way to raise compensation, but is it the most effective in the long term?

Many people are protesting for a nationwide $15/hour, which would raise incomes for women and close the gender gap. What is the magic of that number? Is it the rate that would take a family of four out of poverty on a single income? What if that family has two incomes? What if they have no children? Better yet, why not set the minimum at $250,000/year or at the $428,713 necessary to make every working American a one-percenter?

It is hoped that people would recognize the folly of going that far. What would happen is either inflation would diminish value to the point that $428,713 would buy little more than minimum wage today or most people would lose their jobs, the economy would collapse, and most people would be far worse off.

What about proposals to raise the minimum wage to $11 or $15 per hour?

First, look at the section on Depressed Wages and how, just maybe, the reason compensation hasn't done better has something to do with the economy absorbing over the past 60 years some 29 million more women, 43 million immigrants, and 11 million illegal immigrants. Over the past 18 years, the female workforce participation has flattened out. If we find a way to slow the flow of immigrants to around 500,000 per year, we should see incomes rise without resetting the minimum wage. And if we don't, increasing the minimum wage will make it harder for new immigrants to find jobs, which will be socially disruptive.

However, people want results today.

Consider this. If a single mother making $12/hour gets a raise to $15/hour as part of a nationwide plan, she gets an immediate raise and more money to spend on her family. Now she has to pay someone $15/hour to watch her children. Since she needs to pay the childcare provider from the moment she leaves her children until she returns, she will pay the childcare provider 45 hours a week at $15/hour and receive 40 hours at $15/hour, losing $75/week (5 hours multiplied by $15/hour).

It doesn't stop there. She is required to pay employer payroll taxes for her childcare provider and payroll taxes on her income, so it pays her to stay home and watch her own kids while collecting welfare. Thus, raising the minimum wage will hurt working single mothers.

Ah, but you'll say domestic workers and childcare providers are excluded from the minimum wage laws. What is the rationale? Why fight to raise wages for some and not everyone? Is it not equally important for domestic workers to have a living wage?

There's no question that those who get an increase to $15/hour feel better about their situation. What about those who lose their jobs as a result of a higher minimum wage. Oh, that won't happen. It's just a scare tactic. Look at the section Minimum Wage & Business for an example of what really happens.

The rationale on why job loss won't result goes something like this. Increasing the minimum wage will put more income into the hands of working people, which they will spend on goods and services, which will create jobs.

Sounds like voodoo economics, a variation of trickle-down economics.

It's true that putting more money in the hands of working people will increase their spending and create jobs. However, the additional earnings they will spend didn't just come out of nowhere. It came from their employers, who will have to increase prices and cut costs including employment in order to pay the higher wages. That will reduce spending and jobs elsewhere. This is one of the unfortunate side-effects of forcing a higher minimum wage.

There are those who say that it has been tried in this city or that state without any ill effects, but doing so on a nationwide basis is an entirely different matter. If job growth in that city or state were strong enough to handle the minimum wage increase then the impact would be minimal. When the economy is sluggish, a mandated higher wage would have a different outcome.

The situation for workers who depend on tips will have a similar effect, but they have an even stronger beef when their pay plus tips comes out to less than minimum wage. One solution would be to end tipping and increase base pay so that making less than minimum wage doesn't happen. That would disadvantage those tip earners who currently do well but would help those just scraping by. Efforts should be made so that these workers make at least the minimum wage.

In any case, there will be winners and losers. Those who benefit will say it's worth it. Those who lose their jobs or who have to pay higher prices will complain and no doubt blame their former employers instead of the higher mandated wages.

MINIMUM WAGE & BUSINESS

There are those who say that businesses overstate the impact of minimum wage increases. Let's see what happens down the street at your local McDonalds franchise.

Imagine you're the McDonalds franchise owner who paid $2 million for your business by taking out loans for the full amount (lucky you). You earn $430,000/year which makes you a one-percenter. Of course, you have to repay the $2 million loan over ten years out of your income, which drops your disposable income by $200,000/year. But that's your problem.

Then the government rides in and tells you to raise wages for your 20 employees from $10 to $15 per hour. That will cost you $208,000 ($5/hour additional times 20 employees times 2080 work hours a year). Employer payroll and unemployment taxes take that up to $230,000. The government also tells you to provide health care, which you do at $3,000/employee or another $60,000.

All of a sudden, your income drops from $430,000 to $140,000 (430-230-60=140), all due to new government regulations. And you still owe $200,000 a year in loan payments. That means you don't clear enough to pay the loan let alone cover any of your living costs.

Because your income drops 67% ($430,000 to $140,000), the value of your business drops by that percentage as well, to $650,000. Your business is now under water, like so many mortgages over the past 10 years. Except, you signed a personal guarantee and you can't turn over the keys to the bank and walk away. If you do, the bank gets to grab your house, putting you out on the street.

If you're making $10 an hour working for this guy, you say, "Poor baby, get over it." As the owner, what do you do? Here are your choices:

1. Suck it up and say, "I was greedy before and less income is fair. I'll take out another mortgage on my kids' college education so I can pay off the loan on the business." However, you're not earning enough to ever pay off the mortgage. This won't work.
2. Get out of the business and hope you can salvage your house. Regrettably, you owe $2 million on the loans and your business is only worth $650,000. If you quit, the banks get your business and to make up the difference, they take your home. Thus, you would have to file bankruptcy and take your chances. This doesn't sound good, either.
3. Increase your prices to cover your higher labor costs. You hope other businesses will increase their prices so that you won't lose customers to competition. Even so, higher prices will cause you to lose customers who refuse to pay more. That means less income. Still, raising prices seems a better option than bankruptcy, while you look for other alternatives.
4. Cheapen your product and hope that no one notices the lower grade of meat or the stale buns. You worry that customers will find out. Then you would face a worse prospect, lower sales while you figure out how to get by.
5. Find a way to operate with fewer employees. You consider letting go the day manager. You'll do the job yourself. You consider letting go two workers during the summer and hiring your son and daughter, though you would have to pay them the $15/hour. That won't lower costs, but it will keep money in the family.

As you ponder what to do, an enterprising sales team shows up on your doorstep. They tell you how, for a one-time investment of $100,000 (equipment made in China of course), you can replace four of your $15/hour employees with automated ordering and food processing equipment. Adding in the employer taxes and medical insurance, you can save close to $150,000 per year (4 employees times $15/hour times 2080 work hours a year, plus taxes and insurance).

This sounds much better than losing your business and your house, so you borrow the money on a home equity loan to buy the new equipment. You fire four employees, raise prices less than you otherwise might, and get your income up while you look for other ways to cut costs. You survive while one of your competitors goes out of business, having to let go all his employees.

This is similar to what happened with supermarket cashiers when they went on strike. They got their demands met for higher wages. Then the supermarket brought in barcode scanning and self-service checkouts. Cutting employment offset the cost of higher wages. The money to pay higher wages has to come from somewhere.

If you're one of the employees who keeps your job, your benefit is immediate. You thank the politician who got you the raise. As inflation increases to cover the cost of your higher wages, the creeping price increases never get linked to the wage increase and so you blame greedy businesses, now that your $15/hour wage feels more like $13.

If you're one of the employees who lost your job, your pain is immediate and directed at your former employer, not the politician who legislated the business into paying more. You complain about how unfair business is for putting you out on the street and wait for a candidate to tell you how he or she will fix your problem, while neglecting to tell you of any side-effects.

Supporters of higher minimum wages act as if somehow the rich will pay for the increase out of their own pockets. The underlying assumption is that rich people are stupid. Perhaps stupid rich people may choose to live on lower income until they're broke. But stupid rich people don't stay rich, and when they go broke, their businesses lay off their employees.

No, most decision makers will let employees go or raise prices to offset the cost of mandated changes. That will diminish the value of the higher minimum wage, and bring calls for further increases.

These are the side-effects of increasing the minimum wage. If a city, state, or even national economy is vibrant enough, it can absorb these side-effects. Then again, a vibrant economy doesn't need a minimum wage. Demand for workers will cause wages to rise as it did during the 1960s.

Who pays for the side-effects of a higher minimum wage? That would be the poor, in particular single mothers. What would be more effective would be to encourage businesses to create more jobs and reduce the inflow of immigrants willing to do these jobs for less than minimum wage, since it beats what they have back home.

To those who persist in pushing for an increase in the minimum wage, recognize that the smaller of an increase put in place, the less the dislocation and potential jobs lost. Small increases are less disruptive than a huge increase.

NATIONWIDE MINIMUM WAGE

If a higher minimum wage is a good idea on a local level, why not nationwide?

A national minimum wage is a one-size-fits-all solution to an imbalance in the labor market caused by too many people chasing too few jobs. This problem was created in the first place by outsourcing and by increased workforce participation rates and high immigration, particularly by those willing to work at low wages.

It's true that certain businesses and farms over the years have exploited immigrants for cheap labor. Some have knowingly hired illegal immigrants. Other businesses have looked the other way, despite tighter government mandated checks for illegal immigrants during the hiring process.

This welcoming attitude by businesses and farms has encouraged millions of illegal immigrants to brave dangerous conditions to cross the border. These immigrants come to this country, willing to work at low wages because those low wages are better than what they found at home. What we call exploitation, they see as improving their lives and that of their families; otherwise, they wouldn't keep coming.

Cries for increasing the nationwide minimum wage are loudest in the urban areas since the cost of living is much higher in big cities like New York and San Francisco than in rural areas. Having a higher minimum wage in high cost areas reflects their cost of living, as long as the local economy is dynamic enough to absorb it.

What works in big cities doesn't necessarily work in small towns and rural areas, where costs are much lower.

Applying the same minimum wage across the entire country will change the economic dynamics between regions and between urban and non-urban areas. It would benefit the big cities, where the wage increases would be smallest, at the expense of small towns and rural areas. It would create a monopoly floor to wages that would disproportionately hit non-urban areas and force price inflation in regions with depressed economies and high unemployment.

A side-effect of a nationwide minimum wage would be to shift jobs from non-urban areas to urban areas. With no difference in wages on the low end, certain businesses would choose to be closer to customers as there would be fewer advantages to locating offices and plants in what were previously low wage areas.

Thus, one side-effect of a nationwide minimum wage will be to preserve jobs in the big cities while increasing unemployment in small towns and rural areas.

Perhaps this is a secret wish of those who push for a national rather than a local standard, but a nationwide minimum wage will hurt the less skilled and less trained workers who most need a break to get into the job market. It will also hurt young workers looking for their first jobs.

That's not the end of it. Faced with higher wages, employers will do three things.

1. Increase prices, which will disproportionately hurt the poor.
2. Source jobs outside the country where they don't have a $15 minimum wage, thus increasing unemployment in this country, and hurting the poor.
3. Increase automation to offset higher labor costs, which will hurt the poor.

Faced with a low birth rate and an aversion to immigration, the Japanese have automated as many jobs as they could. For them it worked since it allowed them to function with fewer workers. The United States has not gone that route in part because of immigration and lower wages. Faced with mandated higher wages,

American businesses could adopt more of the technologies already in place in Japan.

Thus, a nationwide $15 minimum wage would benefit those who retain their jobs. It would hurt less skilled workers, workers living in non-urban areas, and young workers seeking their first jobs.

MINIMUM WAGE OPTIONS

The issue of minimum wages comes down to a philosophical question of whether we should let market forces balance available jobs and workers or whether we need to give the market a helping hand.

The latter argument boils down to this: businesses will try to pay the lowest wage they can get away with. In a global economy, they can match up local wages against low wages in other countries and put workers at a disadvantage.

Let's examine the comment that we are now in a global economy. Weren't we in a global economy when tens of millions of people migrated to the United States for better opportunities? Weren't we in a global economy when Irish, Italian, and other immigrants came to these shores willing to work for less than those who came before them?

The only time we were not in a global economy was during the 1930s when we instituted the Smoot-Hawley act and entered a trade war that helped to shrink the U.S. economy and jobs. We also had the lowest immigration rates of the past century. It is hoped that no Americans would wax nostalgic for those days. In any case, yes, we are in a global economy, and have been throughout most of our history.

Here are the underlying facts behind mandating a higher minimum wage. Higher wages encourage more people to enter the job market, while discouraging businesses from creating jobs and hiring. Lower wages discourage people from entering the market, while encouraging businesses to hire.

What are some options to increase low wages in this country?

1. Let market forces balance labor supply against available jobs, allowing lower wages to encourage more hiring. On its own, it could take years for this to raise wages, particularly with our high immigration rates. In conjunction with other actions (such as adjusting immigration rates), market forces will balance out labor supply and demand.
2. Hike the national minimum wage to $15/hour and see what happens. Don't be surprised when smaller towns and rural areas get hit with higher prices and more unemployment.
3. Encourage states and cities to address the minimum wage issue on a local rather than national level. This is closer to where any side-effects would be felt so that local governments can deal with any repercussions.
4. Provide better vocational and technical training to give workers the skills for better jobs.
5. Encourage businesses to create more jobs, which will increase the demand for labor and thereby increase wages.
6. Adopt a Value Added Tax (VAT) that would level the playing field with respect to trade and outsourced jobs, bringing more jobs to America.
7. Focus legal immigration on the needs of the U.S. economy and limit to 500,000 per year.
8. Deal with illegal immigration. (See separate section on Immigration).
9. Address the issue of aging infrastructure by contracting for repairs over a period of time. This would address the infrastructure and employ a number of available workers.
10. Deal with tip based earners who end up making less than minimum wage.
11. Make any changes to the minimum wage gradually to minimize the shock to the economy and allow businesses to adjust to the higher rates.

In any case, without addressing the issues that caused depressed wages, it's unlikely that increasing the minimum wage will have the desired effect.

PART 5: TAXES

≈≈≈≈≈≈≈≈≈≈≈≈≈≈≈≈≈≈

HIGH TAX RATES

One mantra put forth by certain candidates is that high tax rates are compatible with economic growth and will help to fund their programs. What are the facts?

During and after World War II, we had a 90+% top individual income tax rate that began in 1943, continued through the 1950s and up until 1963. This high rate was created to pay for the costs of the war. During the 1950s and up to 1963, the 50% bracket for married couples was at $32,000, which would amount to $240,000 today. At the same time, the corporate tax rate was 52%.

Because of the war, real growth for 1943-44 averaged 12.5%. After the war (1945-49) the economy shrank 2.0% per year. During 1950-53 with the Korean War going on, the economy expanded by an average rate of 6.4%. Over the following 5 years (1954-58), the economy grew only 2.0%, which barely kept up with population growth. From 1959-63, the economy grew at a 4.5% rate. If your eyes are glazing over, here is a simple chart.

	Real Growth	Per Person	
1943-44	12.5%	11.2%	War
1945-49	- 2.0%	- 3.5%	Post-war
1950-53	6.4%	4.7%	War
1954-58	2.0%	0.2%	Post-war
1959-63	4.5%	2.9%	Baby boom

In summary, the 90+% rate was put in place for the war. Economic growth during the war years was spurred by military spending. In the years after World War II and the Korean War, the economy performed poorly on a per capital basis. During 1959-63, the economy did well, spurred by the Baby Boom. For the entire 21 year period, we only have the last 5 years that was not associated with a war and post-war economy. Thus, it would be difficult to conclude that the economy does well with a 90+% tax rate in the absence of war or another Baby Boom.

We had a high tax rate during the 1930s of 63% (1932-35) and 79% (1936-40). The thresholds for the top rates in today's dollars were $17 million and $85 million, respectively. To get to today's 39.6% tax bracket at that time would have required around $1 million of income in today's value.

In 1932, tax rates were increased and the economy had its worst year of the Twentieth century. During 1932-35, the economy only managed to grow at a 1.4% rate or 0.8% per person. This came about with heavy New Deal spending initiatives offsetting any impact of increased taxes. During 1936-38, the economy grew 4.9%, again with New Deal spending initiatives. In 1939-40, the economy grew at an 8.4% rate due to the military buildup to support our allies. See the chart below.

	Real Growth	Per Person	
1932	-12.9%	-13.5%	
1932-35	1.4%	0.8%	New Deal
1936-38	4.9%	4.2%	New Deal
1939-40	8.4%	7.6%	Military buildup

Thus, we saw poor performance during 1932-35, strong performance during 1936-38, and military buildup after that. From 1934 to 1939, the economy did recover off the 26% Depression collapse, though the economy didn't reach 1929 levels until World War II brought the military buildup.

The record of high tax rates is mixed. The 90+% levels were set to pay for World War II and continued until 1963. The high rate in the 1930s may have contributed to the 13% collapse in 1932 and the depths of the Depression. Beyond that the higher taxes in the 1930s were offset by significant New Deal spending initiatives.

In other words, the assertion that the U.S. economy does well under high tax rates without a war rests on shaky ground.

INCREASING TAXES

We've talked about time periods with higher taxes than today. What about the economy's response to tax increases? Other than during wartime, only 5 times in the past century were income tax rates increased.

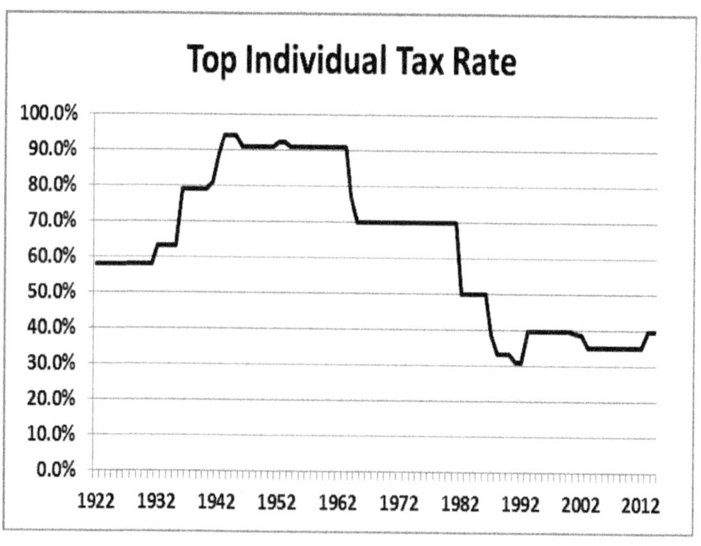

- In 1932, individual tax rates increased with the top rate going from 58% to 63%. At the same time, the corporate tax rate was increased from 12% to 13.75%. Increasing taxes in the middle of the depression helped 1932 become the worse year of the depression, with the economy shrinking 13% that year and another 1% the following year. Not a smart move.

- In 1936, the individual tax rates were increased again with the top rate going to 79% for incomes in today's dollars over $85 million, and increases for everyone making more than $825,000 in today's dollars. The corporate rate also increased to 15%. The economy did well in 1936, slowed in 1937, and went into a 3% decline in 1938.

	Top Individual Tax Rate	Individual Tax % GDP	Real GDP
1988-90	28.0%	7.9%	3.3%
1991-92	31.0%	7.6%	1.7%
1993-95	39.6%	7.6%	3.2%
2003-2012 *	35.0%	7.1%	1.8%
2013-2014	39.6%	8.0%	2.0%

* Included Great Recession

<See Bibliography sources 1, 31>

- In 1991, individual tax rates increased, taking the top rate from 28% to 31% and an overall effective tax increase of about 5%. As compared to 4.1% annual growth from 1983 through 1990, the economy in 1991 was flat and averaged 1.7% growth for 1991-92, which barely kept up with population growth. Despite the higher individual tax rates, individual tax revenue as % of GDP fell from 7.9% prior to the tax increase to 7.6% after. Thus, this rate increase did not increase tax revenues.
- In 1993, individual tax rates increased with the top rate going from 31% to 39.6% and an overall effective increase of about 11%. This time, real GDP (1993-1995) grew an average 3.2%. We didn't include 1997-2000 in this comparison since the capital gains rate dropped in 1997

and the following 4 years exploded with what Alan Greenspan called "irrational exuberance." In any case, the economy did well after a tax rate increase. It should be noted that the new 39.6% rate was still well below the 50% levels of 7 years earlier. This time, individual tax revenue as a percentage of GDP remained at the 7.6% from before the tax increase. In other words, tax revenues didn't go up with the tax rate increase.

- In fact, if we compare the tax increase years of 1991-1995 to the pre-increase years of 1988-90, we find that tax revenues as a percentage of GDP went down from 7.9% to 7.6%. That means the tax rate increase did not increase tax revenues. Also, GDP growth before averaged 3.3% and during 1991-1995 slowed to 2.6%
- In 2013, the individual tax rate increased, taking the top rate from 35% to 39.6%, while leaving other rates the same, for an overall effective tax increase of 2%. GDP growth was 2.1% during the 3 years prior and in the 3 years after this tax increase. Thus, economic growth didn't slow as a result of the tax increase. Individual tax revenue as % GDP grew from 7.1% in the 10 years before to 8.0% in the two years after, though the 13% increase in revenue (8.0 vs. 7.1) can't be explained by a 2% increase in tax rates and so it is too early to evaluate the full impact of the 2013 rate increase, but it appears to have increased tax revenues.

The evidence on increasing taxes is that doing so when the economy is weak, as it was in 1932, seems to have made matters worse. Increasing taxes in 1936 when the economy was rapidly growing may not have stopped the economy, but the income needed to hit the top bracket would have been equivalent to $85 million today. Furthermore, it came after the Depression collapse had depressed the economy and at a time when New Deal spending to stimulate the economy was peaking.

Since World War II, we have had three general individual tax increases (1991, 1993, and 2013). Real GDP dropped after the 1991 tax increase, did much better after the 1993 tax increase, and was flat after the 2013 tax increase. General conclusion: mixed. It is important to note that the highest tax rate during this time was less than 40%, compared to 50% as late as 1986. Increasing taxes above

40% could bring a different dynamic, particularly with a weak economy.

Since one of the purposes of increasing tax rates is to raise more tax revenue, how did that go? After 1991, individual tax revenue went down after the tax rate increase, from 7.9% of GDP to 7.6%. After 1993, this rate remained unchanged at 7.6%. Thus, for the two increases in the 1990s, there was no clear benefit from increasing tax rates. Then in 2013, the individual tax revenue picked up from 7.1% to 8.0%. That can't be accounted for by an effective tax rate increase of 2%. Thus, there is no clear proof that increasing tax rates brings the desired increase in tax revenues.

How can this be?

Simple math says if we double the tax rate, we double the revenue. That makes common sense, but now for some uncommon sense. If you personally were taxed at 50% and your tax rate were doubled to 100%, would you continue to work hard and report your income? Not a chance. No one works for nothing.

Okay, but if your tax rate were 10% and doubled to 20%, you would probably grumble and continue to work. Somewhere in between, taxpayers make personal decisions that affect tax revenues. One example is doctors who cut back their work week to four days. Another is restaurant owners who choose to close for breakfast. These decisions might not be entirely over tax rates, but taxes enter into their decisions. This is a reality that tax-increasers don't like to disclose.

The French recently got a lesson in increasing income tax rates. They raised taxes on high earners with their top rate going to 75%. When tax revenues came in, the government received only half of what they'd calculated they should have collected from their top earners.

Why this happens shouldn't be such a mystery. After governments raise taxes enough, people find ways to avoid having to pay the higher tax. For billionaires, one way is to invest in art instead of job creating businesses. They can experience an increase in their wealth through rising valuations of the art without paying taxes until they sell or die. When they decide to sell, they can have a private sale with no paperwork, nothing reported to the government, and thereby avoid paying taxes. This is illegal, but it isn't only the rich who avoid reporting income.

At a 40% tax rate, there is still enough incentive for taxpayers to invest in job creating businesses, but at some point, higher tax rates provide the incentive for them to avoid income by investing where it doesn't create jobs. That's bad for the economy and for job creation.

Why look at individual tax rates instead of corporate rates when looking at job creation? Small businesses are the engine of job growth. Small business owners typically own their businesses as sole proprietorships, partnerships, S-corporations, and limited liability corporations, all of which are taxed at individual tax rates. They do this to avoid the double taxation as a corporation and then as dividends. If their taxes go up enough, they scale back their efforts, which reduces their income and the jobs they create.

An interesting fact is that during the time of 90+% individual tax rates (1948-63), individual tax revenue averaged 7.2% of GDP. During the period of tax cuts and lower taxes (1964-2014) it averaged 7.9%. Thus, higher tax rates did not lead to higher tax revenues.

So, before you hop on the bandwagon to increase tax rates, particularly above 40%, brace yourself to collect less tax revenue than you expect and take the gamble on economic growth and jobs. The push for higher taxes, above a certain level comes with unintended side-effects.

HISTORY OF CUTTING TAXES

We've talked about the history of high taxes and increasing tax rates. What about when tax rates have decreased?

The table below shows highlights of a 62-year period of general tax rate decreases with a couple of increases:

Trend of Tax Rates, Tax Revenues, and Real GDP					
	Top Tax Rate	Individual Income Tax % GDP	All Taxes	Real GDP	Real GDP per Capita
1952-63	91.2%	7.5%	17.2%	3.4%	3.4%
1964-81	70.4%	7.9%	17.5%	3.6%	3.6%
1982-86	50.0%	8.0%	17.3%	3.5%	3.5%
1987-92	30.8%	7.8%	17.5%	2.8%	2.8%
1993-2002	39.5%	8.5%	18.3%	3.4%	3.4%
2003-12	35.0%	7.1%	16.0%	1.8%	1.8%
2013-2014	39.6%	8.0%	17.1%	2.0%	2.0%
Average	57.4%	7.8%	17.3%	3.1%	3.1%

<See Bibliography sources 1, 31>

Here are some general observations:

- For individual tax rates, the reductions in 1964-65 (15+% overall) and in 1982 (9+% overall) were followed by increases in individual tax revenue as a percentage of GDP. In addition, for these two tax cuts, real GDP per capita went up after the cuts to the highest levels of the 62 year period. Conclusion: cutting individual taxes down to 50% increased tax revenues and helped the economy.
- The individual tax cuts and increases after 1986 seem to show some correlation between increasing or decreasing tax rates and the subsequent individual tax revenues, but only at rates below 40%.
- Overall, the correlation of individual tax rates to tax revenue as a percentage of GDP shows 90+% produced 7.5% revenue, 70% produced 7.9% revenue, 50% produced 8.0% revenue, 39.6% produced 8.4% revenue, and 35% produced 7.1% revenue. This shows that reducing tax rates to approximately 40% increased individual tax revenues. This may be counter-intuitive, but has been demonstrated. Yet, dropping rates below 40% reduced tax revenues. Thus, something around 40% maximizes individual tax revenues.

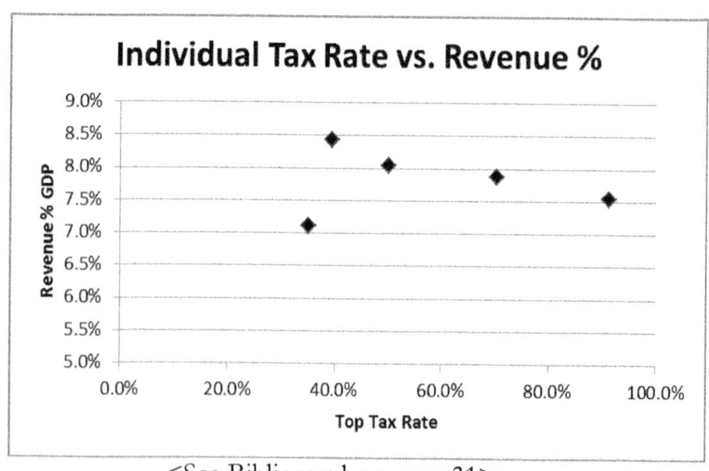

<See Bibliography source 31>

- In addition, individual tax cuts below 39.6% did not show any improvement in real GDP per capita.
- For corporate tax rates, the reductions from 1963 to 1982 represented 12% lower rates and a 70% reduction in tax revenue as a percentage of GDP. Since businesses pay taxes on net income after deducting all business expenses, this implies that there has been a rapid expansion of additional business subsidies such as the corn-ethanol and solar energy incentives, and accelerated oil depletion.
- The corporate tax rate dropped again in 1988 to mid-30s%, after which corporate tax revenue increased from 1.3% to 1.8%, but still well below the levels prior to 1982. Because of the complexity of corporate taxation, this will take further study.

What about the last two tax reductions?

- In 1987-88, individual tax rates dropped with the top rate going from 50% to 28% and most Americans receiving a tax cut. Individual tax revenues went up slightly from 7.8 to 7.9%. However, the tax cut was from 50%, meaning the impact could have been from dropping the rate from 50% to say 40% and not all the way down to 28%. The economy slowed, yet was still running at 3.3% (2.2% per capita).
- In 2002-03, individual tax rates dropped from a maximum of 39.1% to 35%, with an effective overall tax rate decrease of 12%. Individual tax revenues plunged 14% from 8.5% (1993-2000) to 7.3% (2003-07) and real GDP slowed.

Thus, the 1987-88 tax rate cut was in line with the tax cuts in 1964-65 and in 1982 in preserving tax revenues and helping the economy, but possibly because it was coming off a 50% rate. The 2002-03 tax cut did not spur the economy and hit dollar-for-dollar against the deficit with no apparent economic benefit.

Overall conclusions relative to individual tax cutting are that cutting the tax rate down to around 40% has increased individual tax revenue and has been good for economic growth. Reducing rates below that level has reduced tax revenue and has not shown any benefit in growth.

Granted there are only a few data points, but while this does not support cutting taxes from current levels, it also does not support the predicted benefits of increasing tax rates, either.

RATIONAL TO INCREASE/CUT TAXES

While we can debate the philosophical and ideological reasons as to why we want higher or lower taxes, history does not support either move from the 39.6% current individual tax rate levels.

Those who follow the mantra of "soak the rich" seek to reduce the concentration of wealth and income. Yet, as demonstrated in the sections on Billionaires, increasing income and estate taxes will not address billionaire wealth concentration. Other people, in line with wanting more equal wealth distribution want to increase taxes on all those who make more than they do, which is a form of envy unless it serves another benefit than dragging other people down.

The other benefit anticipated by tax-increasers is as a means to raise more government revenue to cover spending initiatives. As shown in the section History of Cutting Taxes, except during a major military conflict like World War II where all Americans were engaged, and where military spending boosted the economy, whenever we have had high individual tax rates, revenue from those taxes has been lower as a percentage of GDP.

The reality is that increasing tax rates pulls money out of the productive economy and turns it over to the consuming economy in the hope and prayer that increased consumption will trickle down to more jobs. One side-effect of increasing tax rates above 40% is that tax revenues do not go up with the rate increase.

People will point to the 1993 and 2003 tax increases and say, "Not so." Those increases were to less than 40%, which was below the rates in effect from 1964-81. The 1990s boomed under a tax structure well below that in place from 1945 through 1986. It's something to think about.

Then there are those who cherish lower taxes.

The philosophical premise for lowering tax rates is that money belongs to the people and not to the government. The smallest government is the best. The first and most important of the government's roles is to keep our citizens safe from foreign threats (defense/military spending). What about roads, airports, bridges, and other infrastructure? What about the entire structure of interstate and international trade whereby we sell products and services beyond our borders? What about a common basis of currency that we all get paid in and depend on?

Government isn't free.

We can debate as to what services the national government should perform relative to the states and local governments, but that debate needs to be had before we start cutting taxes. The idea of "starve the beast" has helped to bring about growing debt levels that are and will continue to hurt economic growth well into the future. The interest expense on the enormous debt is a drag on the economy.

This is not a philosophical debate but a cliff we are driving over. There will be serious side-effects of cutting taxes without cutting federal spending at a time when most of the government funds goes to Social Security, Medicare, interest expense on the enormous debt, and defense.

Aside from the reality that none of us likes paying taxes and would be delighted if we could have all the benefits of citizenship without having to pay, the entire rationale for cutting taxes for economic benefit is based on improving incentives to the productive sector and thus spurring the economy.

Despite critics who would like to say otherwise, these benefits were demonstrated in the 1960s and in the 1980s with those tax cuts down to 50%. History supports this. On the other hand, the 2002-03 tax cuts did not provide benefits and instead increased the national debt without boosting the economy.

The historical evidence supports bringing the top individual tax rate down to 50% and most likely to 40%. The evidence does not support further tax cuts and instead points to side-effects of increasing federal deficits without spurring economic growth. This has to do with the diminishing returns of cutting taxes.

DIMINISHING RETURNS OF CUTTING TAXES

Some people advocate lower taxes on the premise that putting more money in the hands of the people will stimulate the economy and create jobs. Does this really work?

There has been much talk about the benefits of lowering taxes. As mentioned in the History of Cutting Taxes, there is strong evidence that reducing taxes in the past from rates above 50% has been followed by economic growth for several years. If this is so, why not reduce taxes to 10% or eliminate taxes altogether?

For one thing, an individual tax rate paid by everyone at less than 13-15% won't cover the Federal budget, which is already heavily in debt. Federal spending is over 20% of GDP. The immediate effect of reducing taxes without reducing Federal spending is to increase the national debt. While individuals would have more money to spend, the debt puts pressure on interest rates and borrowing that offsets the impact of additional money to spend.

If the government spends less in order to balance the budget, then those who directly or indirectly receive paychecks from the government will have less to spend. When they spend less, those they would have bought from have to lay people off.

Cutting taxes doesn't come free.

The only real economic rationale for reducing taxes is that under certain circumstances (starting with high tax rates) reducing the rates provides incentives for businesses to expand and create jobs. Since many small businesses are sole proprietorships, partnerships, S-corporations, and limited liability corporations that get taxed as individuals, it is the individual tax rate that influences the decisions of small businesses, not corporate rates.

How does the additional economic incentive for small businesses square with the drop in individual tax rates?

The 1964-65 tax cut dropped the top bracket from 91% to 70%. Even the $1 million bracket (today's dollars) dropped from 81% to 66%. This represented an increase in after-tax income to the top taxpayers of 233% (from 9% to 30%) and for the $1 million earners of 79% (from 19% to 34%). This more than tripled the investment incentive for top earners and nearly doubled it for the lower group. For the top group, the tax revenue dropped by 23% (70/91). 1964-69 was one of the strongest periods of real economic growth, averaging 4.9%/year.

The 1982 tax cut dropped the top bracket from 70% to 50%. This amounted to an increase in after-tax income of 67% (from 30% to 50%), still a healthy investment incentive. At the same time, tax revenue from this group dropped by 29% (50/70). The economy averaged 4.9%/year real growth from 1983-86.

Then in 1987-88, the top tax bracket was cut from 50% to 28%, an increase in after-tax income of 44% (from 50% to 72%), which was a smaller incentive, though still significant. Tax revenue from this group dropped by 44% (28/50). In response, the economy grew an average 3.8% per year over the next three years. Thus, the incentive to the top income group was the least, the tax loss the greatest, and the economic benefit was good though less than in the earlier time periods. This is called the law of diminishing returns.

The 2002-03 tax reduction from 39.6% to 35% provided an increase in after-tax income of 7.6% (from 60.4% to 65%) and a reduction in tax revenue from this group of 11.6% (35/39.6). It was hardly worth the trouble. Even so, the economy from 2002 to 2007 grew at a 2.9% annual rate, while having to deal with the economic dislocation and uncertainties following 9/11. Was this related to the minor tax reduction or the Federal Reserve's easy money put in place after 9/11?

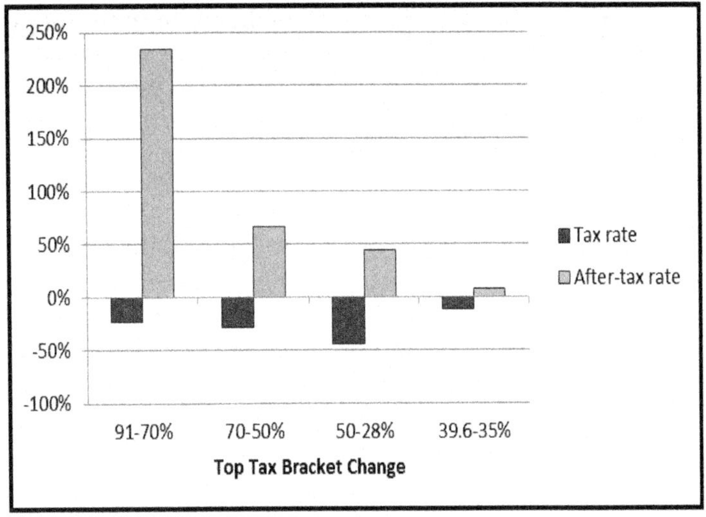

The chart above shows the impact of diminishing returns. As the rates drop, the benefits of the next cut to small businesses and individuals shrinks, and the incentives to stimulation the economy drop. Cutting from 91% and from 70% offered large investment incentives and were followed by strong economic growth. The benefits of tax reduction came from reducing the top rate to 40%. Beyond that, the benefits of further tax cutting diminish.

The loss of tax revenue is smallest when cutting from a high tax rate at the same time that the incentive for small businesses to create new jobs is highest. Cutting from lower levels means a large loss in tax revenue for a small incentive to small businesses. The sweet spot seems to be around 40%.

As an illustration, a rate drop from 39.6% to 15% would represent an increase in after-tax income of 41% (85% vs. 60.4%) and a decrease in tax revenues of 62% (15/39.6) from this group. If this came about as part of moving to a flat tax, the decrease in tax revenues could be softened or eliminated by removal of tax loopholes. The incentives in general would remain at 41%, but incentives for lost tax loopholes would vanish, leading to diminished economic activities in those areas.

If this came as part of another general tax cut, there would be a short term adjustment to the economy as people would have more money to spend. Then the burden of additional debt would stifle economic growth as has happened over the past 15 years.

In any case, the reason certain wealthy people were unfazed by a reversal of the Bush tax cuts was that those only represented a 7.6% impact on after tax income (65% vs. 60.4%). It wasn't enough to sway business or personal spending decisions, though it did add to the debt.

In summary, the tax cuts in the 1960s and 1980s had economic incentive as a motive and were followed by strong economic growth. Those who point to those benefits as justifying further cuts are running up against the law of diminishing returns.

Cutting taxes below 39.6% provided minimal incentive, little economic benefit, and the side-effect of additional government debt. This does not support further tax cuts.

CAPITAL GAINS TAX

One political mantra calls the capital gains tax a rich man's tax that should be at a higher rate. It feels right, so it must be. Right?

This has also been called an "entitlement" to the rich. So, how did we get to a lower tax rate on capital gains, other than the rich guys want it?

The capital gains tax rate applies to assets held for at least one year and then sold. Let's say you bought an antique table for $1,000 and kept it for 10 years during which general inflation increased prices by 25%. Let's say you sell the table for $1,250. According to the IRS, you have a gain of $250 that gets taxed at the capital gains rate. Do you really have a gain?

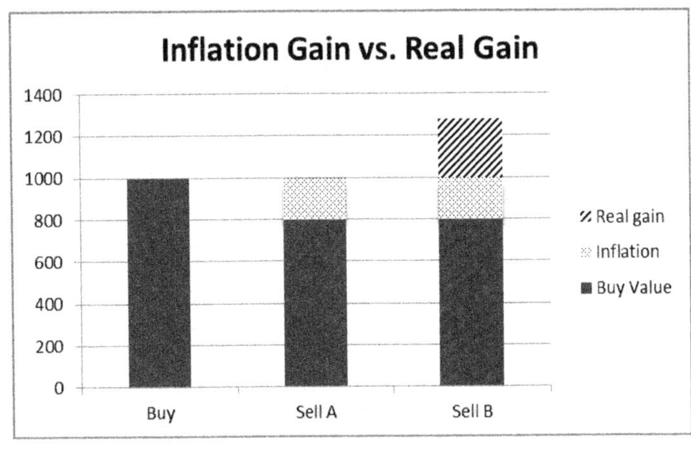

Your $1,250 today holds the same value as the $1,000 you paid 10 years ago. All you have done is preserve your money. You've sold the table for the same value of food, clothing, gas, etc. as when you bought it. You don't have any more spending value. Yet, the government says you must pay a tax. When you do, you will be left with less value than you had 10 years ago.

Let's take the same circumstances except that after 10 years you sell that table for $1,600. You have a $600 taxable gain of which $250 covers the 25% inflation on your original purchase. You have a $350 real gain in value.

Should you pay the same tax on your inflation recovery as you do on your real gain and on ordinary wage income? That is the question.

To charge the full, ordinary income tax rate on the entire increase in price is to tax the inflation on your money, which inflation the government controls through its fiscal and monetary policies. Thus was born the reduced tax rate for capital gains to reflect that part of the gain is just recovery of inflation.

On the other hand, hedge funds take advantage of the lower capital gains rate. They invest in companies they often hold for only a few years, during which there is little inflation. Yet, they get the same benefit of the reduced tax rate as someone who holds their assets for decades.

One option that more directly removes the hedge fund advantage while not taxing the inflation recovery would be to index investment costs so that the $250 inflation recovery would receive no tax and the $350 real gain would be taxed at the ordinary tax rate.

DIVIDEND TAX

Here we have another case of what has been called the rich man's tax and by some an "entitlement" to the rich. Why should dividends get a preferential tax rate?

The simple answer is double taxation.

Dividends are paid out of corporation earnings. Corporations are already subject to a general 35% tax on their income. Yes, there are a few mega-multinational corporations who play games by moving their income to other countries with lower tax rates. They also park profits in other countries to defer paying U.S. taxes until profits are returned to the U.S. These issues should be addressed directly at the corporation level, not through the dividend tax since not all corporations pay dividends.

Some corporations pay less tax this year because of losses in prior years. Others receive special tax incentives for producing ethanol, investing in solar power, or making certain other government favored investments: a long list of loopholes favoring one business activity over others. Still, the corporate tax rate is 35% and most corporations pay that on reportable income.

Then they pay out dividends that are taxed to individuals at as high as 20%. Combining the two taxes yields a 48% tax rate. Thus, people in the highest tax bracket are already paying an effective 48% tax rate on corporate earnings through dividends. If their tax rate was increased to the maximum ordinary rate of 39.6%, then their effective tax rate would be 61%. If the individual tax rate was increased to 52% as one candidate proposes, then the top effective tax rate on dividends would be 69%.

With the current combined top tax rate at 48% being so much higher than the top individual tax rate of 39.6%, why should corporate income/dividend double taxation be any higher.

TAX LOOPHOLES

Proponents of higher taxes talk about closing tax loopholes. The proponents of lower taxes talk about closing tax loopholes. Yet, they don't agree on which loopholes. What gives?

The idea of loopholes or "tax expenditures" as some people like to call them derives from the Medieval concept that all property and income belongs to the crown or feudal lord and by the grace of our esteemed rulers they let us keep some. One of the reasons that some candidates prefer high tax rates is that it allows them to pick winners and losers in terms of who gets tax breaks (loopholes) against those high rates.

Flat tax advocates say we should eliminate most or all tax breaks (loopholes) and have a lower tax rate paid by all. They make the case that we should let the market decide where investments get made instead of bureaucrats in Washington. Unfortunately, everyone wants an exception for their own pet project. One person's loophole is another person's incentive. Every single one of these "tax expenditures" was created as an incentive to change taxpayer behavior and to help the favored few of the politicians who vote for them.

Home ownership is good for Americans and for the country, plus it helps to build the middle class, so the government encourages more. We have loopholes that allow homeowners to deduct interest expense and real estate taxes in arriving at their taxable income. Thus, part of their housing costs is subsidized by tax breaks. The interest deduction alone is worth about $75 billion a year. This benefits primarily the middle class.

By the way, this loophole along with easy credit encourages people to buy bigger and more expensive homes than they otherwise could have afforded. It does this by reducing the net after-tax cost of interest and real estate taxes. After all, when people look at the affordability of buying a house, they look at their mortgage payment (including interest and real estate taxes) against their after-tax disposable income (after their tax deductions for interest and real estate taxes).

This has the unfortunate side-effect of driving up house prices to levels that many Americans can't afford. It also contributes to housing bubbles that turn home ownership into speculative investments. When combined with the easy mortgages prior to 2008, the tax-subsidized interest led to a boom and then bust in real estate prices and the economy in general.

Bear in mind that Americans owned homes before this tax loophole was put into place. Yet, eliminating this loophole carries a significant risk of causing another collapse in the real estate market, which has struggled to recover from the 2007-09 collapse. One way to soften the blow would be to reduce the home interest deduction over a ten-year period by half or to zero at the same time as reducing tax rates to soften the blow of removing the loophole.

The real estate industry will vehemently oppose removing these deductions in order to protect their livelihoods. Even if overall taxes don't change, taxpayers will feel that they've given up more in losing the tax deductions than they gain in lower rates that could ratchet up in future.

Retirement planning is a good thing. That's why we have loophole incentives in the way of 401k, IRA, and other deductible savings and pension plans, which are worth upwards of $100 billion a year. The idea is to get people to save for their own retirements. Removing these deductions would primarily hurt the middle class, because of limits on contributions by the rich.

One of the biggest tax loopholes is health insurance premiums and cost deductions. This loophole is estimated to be worth $150 billion a year. Companies get to deduct their cost of medical premiums while workers don't have to pay taxes on their benefits. This was a victory of politics over reality that began during World War II. As mentioned earlier, this arrangement has led to skyrocketing medical costs. Removing this loophole would primarily hurt the middle class and poor.

College education is a key to advancement in our society. Helping people to pay the enormous costs of education is a good thing. To help, we have student loopholes such as the 529 College Savings Plan, the Coverdell Education Savings Accounts, the Lifetime Learning Credit, and the American Opportunity Tax Credit. If these went away, they would hurt students.

To those with low incomes, we have tax loopholes to help them out. These include the Earned Income Tax Credit, which costs the government some $70 billion a year in lost tax revenue. Obviously, removing this credit would devastate the poor. Another loophole for the poor is the Retirement Saver's Tax Credit that doubles as incentive to save for their retirements.

Green energy has been deemed a societal benefit and so we have several green energy loopholes. Those include tax credits for using fuel cells and for installing solar energy systems, residential wind turbines, geothermal heat pumps, insulated windows and doors, energy efficient non-solar water heaters, and reflective roofs. These incentives primarily benefit the middle class because of limits on deductions for the rich.

Supposedly to reduce our dependence on oil and our carbon emissions, but mostly to help corn farmers, we have the corn-ethanol subsidies. We have this despite the fact that corn is not the clean ethanol source that sugar cane is. Unfortunately, sugar cane doesn't grow in the Corn Belt. Still, the loophole does help farmers. Also to help farmers, we have a host of subsidies, including the sugar subsidy that benefits farmers at the expense of American consumers.

Other personal loopholes include the deduction for state and local taxes, which is worth about $60 billion a year. The idea behind this was that the Federal government shouldn't be raising taxes on the taxes paid to state and local governments. Removing this deduction would hurt the middle class and the upper middle class. The wealthy lose this deduction already through a phase-out of deductions.

Another loophole is for charitable donations. The idea was to incentivize people to make donations to worthwhile charities. Removing this deduction would primarily hurt the middle class since deductions are phased out for the wealthy.

Bear in mind that the American people never get to vote on these loopholes. If put to a public vote, there are probably few loopholes that would receive 51% vote of all Americans. These giveaways are doled out piecemeal to benefit one group or another at the expense of all Americans.

Everyone seems to have loopholes they would fight for and others they would like to have removed. The flat-tax people propose to make them all go away and reduce rates so that the loss of the loopholes wouldn't amount to as much. Still, the powerful lobbies for loopholes will fight any attempt to eliminate their little goodie.

The right answer would be to put various proposals to the American people—a lower rate with no loopholes or a higher rate with. That isn't going to happen. In the end, there is a powerful group behind each loophole, which is why they have all been preserved.

FAIR SHARE OF TAXES

Are the rich paying their fair share of taxes?

The political mantra is that the "rich" do not pay their fair share and thus need to pay more. That depends on what the speaker means by "fair share." If you're struggling to get by, you may feel that those who earn more than you need to pay more.

What are the facts?

The share of income taxes paid by the bottom 90% of taxpayers has dropped from a high of 52% in 1980 to 27% in 2011 and 30% in 2013 at a time when tax rates were coming down that some say only benefitted the rich. How could the cuts only benefit the rich when the bottom 90% of taxpayers pays a much smaller share of income taxes than in the past?

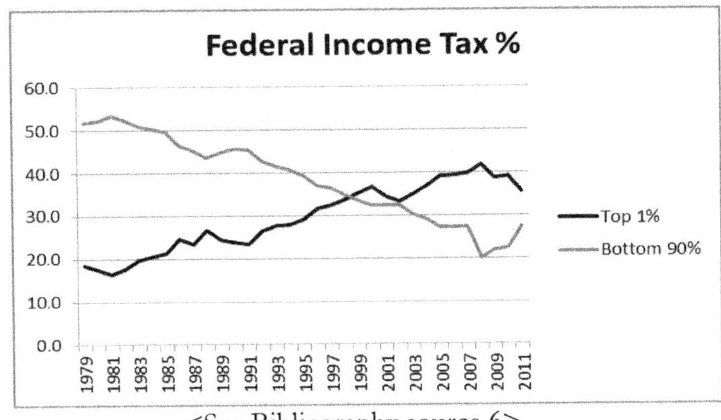

<See Bibliography source 6>

According to the Tax Policy Center, 45% of American households paid no federal income tax in 2014. This is due to a number of tax credits such as the Earned Income Credit, the Child Credit, and many more. Certainly people who pay no income tax can't complain that they're paying an unfair share.

It's true that many of those who pay no federal income tax do pay payroll taxes along with their employers. These taxes help cover a portion and only a portion of their own personal Social Security retirement and Medicare benefits. Asking to not have to pay payroll taxes is like going into a car dealership and demanding a brand new car for free.

No one likes to pay taxes. Yet, of all the taxes we have to pay, this is the only one for which we are paying in for our own benefit. Those who pay general taxes do so for a host of spending that doesn't benefit them personally as well as those that do, but Social Security and Medicare are personal benefits that we directly pay for through payroll taxes. Unless you die young, none of the money you put into payroll taxes goes to anyone but yourself.

Reducing or eliminating payroll taxes makes no sense in this light, above all since individuals pay less than half of their own benefits (matched by employers) and the balance is already subsidized by the rich through general taxes. Besides, the Tax Policy Center goes on to say that 27% of American households pay no net federal income and payroll taxes, after refundable tax credits. Certainly these people can't complain that they are being overtaxed.

While the share of income taxes paid by the bottom 90% has dropped from 52% to 27%, the share paid by the top 1% has grown from 17% in 1980 to 35% in 2011 and 38% in 2013. Even so, the tax-increasers repeat their mantra that tax cuts only benefitted the top 1% and they are not paying their fair share.

What this data means is that the top 1% pay 38% of the national defense budget and 38% of Federal spending on education, veterans benefits, health (excluding Medicare), subsidies for underfunded Medicare, and the judicial system. Meanwhile, 45% of Americans pay nothing for these services.

So, when candidates repeat the mantra that the one-percenters are not paying their fair share, it simply isn't true. How much more would be "fair" to satisfy the tax-increasers and is this about fairness or envy?

High income individuals have faced higher tax rates in the past, particularly during and after wartime, such as the 90+% used to pay for World War II. As has been shown elsewhere, high taxes rates have been associated with lower tax revenues, and often with a sluggish economy and slow job growth that hurt lower income families.

Fairness appears to be a slogan to flash about in order to raise taxes to pay for new or expanded programs. However, raising tax rates above 40% has not been shown to increase tax revenues.

TAX PROPOSALS

What are some of the tax schemes floating around?

One proposal calls for a 15% tax credit for companies that share profits with employees. This will become another tax loophole. It will benefit those companies that already share profits with their workers, giving those companies a tax benefit without changing behavior or helping the workers.

The proposal may encourage other companies who are on the fence about profit sharing, but at 15%, it's not enough incentive to get reluctant companies to participate. The math doesn't work for paying out $1000 in profit sharing to get a $150 tax credit and a deduction that at 35% would save $350 in taxes. The company would still be out $500. If they're reluctant, that won't persuade them. Also, it may encourage companies to pay less in salaries over time as an offset to what is paid out in profit sharing, defeating the purpose of this proposal.

Other candidates propose that we eliminate the current complicated tax structure, which favors the wealthy who can afford tax lawyers and accountants. Their proposal is a 10-15% flat tax with a hurdle to protect the poor and lower-middle class. One version of this would be a simplified income tax that would eliminate all loopholes and could be done on a single sheet of paper.

The biggest downside to simplifying the tax system is that it removes the opportunity for certain politicians and government officials to grant special privileges to their friends. Special interests will continue to pour money into Washington to keep their privileges. The advantage of lower tax rates in exchange for no loopholes is that there would be less advantage to special interests to push for loopholes against a 15% tax than against a 35% tax.

In reality, most of the flat-tax plans are not revenue neutral. The cost of these plans is huge and often accompanied by proposed cuts in Federal spending and the expectation that lower taxes will stimulate the economy. It has already been shown that reducing tax rates below the current 39.6% top rate provides limited economic incentives and has not been shown to help the economy. The primary effect has been increased debt levels.

The simplified flat income tax is presented as a fair tax, but unless it excludes income below a certain hurdle, it will represent an increase on the poor. Therefore, it already has two brackets (zero and the agreed to rate).

From its very beginning, over a hundred years ago, the tax system has had multiple levels, reflecting that wealthier individuals can afford to pay more than the poor and middle class. The question of how much more has long been debated, but it's not clear what the rationale would be for a single flat tax other than to benefit the rich. Thus, using a single flat rate doesn't appear consistent with American history or values. Perhaps a gradual sliding scale with 3-4 tiers and no loopholes would make more sense.

Some candidates propose eliminating the payroll tax to curry favor with voters who pay little or no income tax but are burdened by the payroll tax. As discussed under the Social Security section, payroll taxes with its employer match only pay a portion of retirement benefits for most American workers and yet, this is our personal contribution to our own retirement plan. As noted elsewhere, unless you die young, none of the money you pay in payroll taxes goes to anyone but yourself.

The only people who pay their own Social Security retirement benefits through payroll taxes and employer match are those who earn close to or above the maximum of $118,500/year over their working careers. Those people also make up the difference for those who earn less through general income taxes. To remove the payroll tax and have it paid out of general taxes would be to admit that Social Security doesn't belong to the workers but is no more than another subsidized entitlement program.

Finally, some of the flat-tax plans seek to eliminate the individual and business income taxes and replace them with what sounds like a Value Added Tax (VAT), which is a form of national sales tax. Actually, reducing income taxes and replacing them with a VAT isn't such a bad idea as long as other taxes are reduced for a revenue neutral solution. Otherwise, the net tax increase would be a drag on the economy and on job creation.

One of the greatest benefits of replacing income taxes with a VAT is that it would level the playing field with respect to international trade. It would do so without bringing a trade war since most of our trading partners already use the VAT.

Currently on imports, the only tax the Federal government collects is income taxes on profits deemed made in the United States, which is only a portion of the profits on the sale. Under a VAT, the imports would be subject to taxes on 100% of the amount sold.

On exports, American companies currently have to pay income taxes on what they produce and then when they sell overseas, they have to pay VAT to foreign countries. If a VAT replaced income taxes, exports would not be subject to any U.S. tax and would be cheaper and better able to compete for sales overseas.

The current system encourages imports and discourages exports. Replacing income taxes with a VAT would discourage imports and encourage exports. That would boost U.S. manufacturing and bring jobs back to America. Perhaps we could bring back some of the 3.2 million jobs that went to China.

This move will only benefit the U.S. economy if the overall tax revenue remains about the same, since a net tax increase will slow economic growth.

ESTATE/DEATH TAXES

How high of a death tax would be fair and equitable?

The current estate tax begins on estates above $5.43 million and carries a top rate of 40% on estates $1 million above this. Thus, the 40% rate applies to estates above $6.43 million. In 1965, the exemption was only $60,000 (equivalent to $464,000 today) and their 39% tax rate applied to estates over $1 million above this (equivalent to $7.74 million today). Thus, in 1965 the 39% rate applied to estates above $8.2 million.

Some candidates propose taxing estates as low as $3.5 million in order to get the billionaires or the one-percenters. It takes almost $8 million to be classified as a one-percenter in 2013. Thus, going after smaller estates has nothing to do with taxing billionaires or the one-percenters.

The argument for no death tax is that this tax forces family owners of small businesses and farms to sell their businesses upon the death of one owner in order to pay this tax. Otherwise, those family members have to borrow heavily in order to pay this tax and hold onto the business. The closing or sale of small businesses leads to loss of jobs and the consolidation of small businesses into much larger ones, which lead to consolidation of wealth.

On the other side is the argument that for a democratic society to thrive requires that all citizens be born equal, or at least have similar opportunities. After all, in the eyes of God, we are all created equal, even if we choose not to see that. Passing wealth along to the next generation gives the children of wealth advantages that threaten the equal opportunity upon which our democracy is built. In fact, while the Founding Fathers were entrepreneurial with respect to business in this country, they feared inherited wealth as a precursor to the European aristocracies that they despised and fought against.

Complicating this discussion is human nature. People have a strong motivation to work hard to improve their lot and that of their children. This incentive to work hard and leave something behind for their families is a valuable cornerstone of a strong democracy. In addition, a free democratic society based on free enterprise cannot consider itself free and at the same time confiscate the benefits created by the hard work of its citizens over their lifetimes.

How can we balance these opposing views?

1. In a democracy we should all be born equal. It runs counter to democratic values for concentration of wealth to get passed on to a selected few of the next generation, giving them advantages not available to all.
2. The motivation to excel and contribute to this society comes in large part from its citizens' desire and efforts to pass on benefits to their offspring, to help their offspring to have a better life than they had. Removing such incentive will remove the entrepreneurial spirit that has created so many jobs in this country.

Since the wealth concentration and inherited wealth that we keep hearing about that is most damaging to our concept of equality is in the billionaires, why not put the focus on them or even at the $100 million level? The majority of small businesses that would be threatened with having to be broken up would be in the under $10 million sized estates.

One solution would be to exclude estates under $10 million from estate taxes and have a graduated scale above that balances the two opposing views. This approach would provide the family business incentive while limiting the concentration of extreme inherited wealth between generations.

While this proposal has much merit, there are two ways that billionaires can avoid paying estate taxes if they perceive the rates to be too high. First, they can make charitable contributions. More specifically, they can set up charitable foundations, as many billionaires have, into which they put their money to be administered during their lifetimes and after their deaths in the manner in which they choose.

This money is excluded from estate taxes. Unfortunately, removing this estate tax loophole would hurt many beneficial charities along with the billionaire foundations. In addition, many of these foundations do significant good for society in terms of funding research and efforts to eradicate disease. The good news from the standpoint of inherited wealth is that this wealth is not going to their offspring.

Second, billionaires can move their residence and citizenship to a tax haven country to avoid the taxes if they decide the cost of the tax exceeds the benefits of U.S. citizenship and residence.

There is a third way they can avoid taxes. They can marry a younger spouse and give their estate tax-free to their spouse. When the first spouse dies, the survivor can marry a younger spouse and indefinitely avoid paying estate taxes unless they both die together.

A related proposal to the estate tax would remove the step-up basis. This takes some explanation. When you buy and sell an asset (a stock, a house, a piece of art), the amount you pay for it is called the basis. When you sell, you owe tax on the difference between what you sold it for and the basis. When you die, the basis gets reset to the value at the time of death. While an estate tax may be due on the value of the estate, no income tax is due on the gain at the time of death and when the beneficiary sells, he or she pays taxes on the difference between the selling price and the stepped-up basis.

This proposal calls for eliminating the step up. That could be handled in one of two ways: 1) have the beneficiary use the same basis as the donor and pay the tax when he sells, or 2) have a capital gains tax due at time of his death. The first is consistent with current capital gains and other tax law in that no tax is due until the asset is sold. The second would put a burden on the estate to pay additional taxes at the time of death. Maybe this works for billionaires, but in the small business example, this will put additional pressure to sell small businesses at the time of death, forcing a consolidation into ever bigger companies. Is that really what we want?

In summary, perhaps it makes sense to increase tax rates on estates above $100 million to reduce the impact of significant inherited wealth in giving a select few of the next generation an unfair advantage. This would address a concern of our Founding Fathers that significant inherited wealth could lead to an American aristocracy along the lines of those they saw in Europe. It would also address the issue that significant inherited wealth is at odds with the equal opportunity that underlies an effective democracy.

It should be noted that, unlike the billionaires, estates of $3.5 million in no way represent a risk to democracy or the risk of becoming an aristocracy. Far from it, they represent the success of a free and entrepreneurial society. Perhaps it is time for candidates to stop confusing millions with billions and trillions.

PART 6: ECONOMICS

≈≈≈≈≈≈≈≈≈≈≈≈≈≈≈≈≈≈≈≈≈≈≈≈

SOCIALIST MODEL

Socialism has great appeal to those who find themselves suffering and in need. It offers increased income and benefits and asks nothing in return except for political support. To each according to their needs; from each according to their abilities. What's not to like?

The core premise of socialism is taking from the "rich" however that is defined and giving to the constituents who support socialist leaders. It sounds a lot like Robin Hood with some serious flaws. First of which is that the mythical Robin Hood practiced his craft in a tiny community, not in a nation of 320 million people.

History has shown us that socialism destroys initiative. Think of it this way. If you joined the arduous task of chopping down trees for firewood along with 99 other family members and friends, and you doubled your efforts, you would only receive 1% more firewood for your exertions. Still, you would be helping people you know and care about. Your true benefit is not only the additional firewood you get to enjoy, but also watching your friends and family do better. In addition, your example and peer pressure would encourage others to pitch in, raising the benefits to the group. This is the power of family and small communities.

How would that work if you didn't know the 99 other people? Let's say they live across the country. Would you work twice as hard for people you don't know and will never meet? Perhaps you're altruistic enough to embrace receiving only a 1% additional benefit and the knowledge you're helping others.

Unless you are connected to these others, which would put you in the first example, you don't get to see the benefit of your extra labors. Furthermore, unless you're a celebrity, you don't get to motivate the others to work harder for the group. Thus, you're not able to use peer pressure to get others to work harder so that everyone benefits.

Let's say you have to share your benefits with 320 million strangers, which makes your contribution even more impersonal than in a nation of 5 million such as Denmark or Norway. For the sake of this discussion, assume that your normal efforts provide you an income of $40,000, the same as everyone else in your egalitarian society. By working evenings and weekends, you come up with a way to double your results.

In an entrepreneurial society, working harder and smarter would enable you to double your income. In an oligopoly, the benefits of working harder/smarter get shared with the oligarchs. In a socialist environment with 320 million other people, your reward for ingenuity would be less than one cent over your entire lifetime. If you don't believe me, try dividing $40,000 by 320 million and multiplying the result by your life expectancy.

Your hope is that you could convince 320 million strangers to do the same. Getting that many people to agree on anything is doubtful. Would you make the effort or kick back and enjoy your extra time? What would be your incentive?

As perhaps a more poignant example, imagine a simplified society where one-third of the people earned $60,000 per year and the other two-thirds earned $30,000. Into this society comes a redistributionist-egalitarian who says no one should have more than anyone else. The new leader wins in a landslide (two-thirds) and taxes the one-third $20,000 each, distributing the new tax among the two-thirds as promised. Now everyone has equal after-tax income at $40,000.

For a year.

Seeing that they can't make any more money working 40 hours than by working 27, the one-third decide to cut back their hours so that they earn the $40,000 they will be allowed to keep. After all, why work longer hours for no more benefit when you can skip work and enjoy your free time. The two-thirds realize that working full time gives them no more benefits than working part time and so they find jobs where they can work shorter hours for less pay.

In the real world, what keeps people from slacking off is peer pressure from their co-workers and community, but when you and your co-workers can go fishing instead of working harder with the expectation of the same income, why work?

So, what happens?

In year two, the one-third earns $40,000. The two-thirds earn $27,000. The society's average is now $31,000. Fearless leader taxes the rich one-third $9,000 and redistributes to the poor two-thirds and everyone is worse off.

Simply put, socialism destroys the incentive of individuals, families, and small groups to work harder to improve themselves when their gains will be redistributed to anonymous others, particularly in a large, diverse society like the United States.

SOCIALIST EXPERIENCE

Those people who promote socialism like to point to socialist "successes" in other countries. Top of the list are countries like Denmark, Norway, Finland, and Sweden, the Scandinavian countries, all of which have populations of less than 10 million and until recently were homogeneous societies with limited diversity. It remains to be seen how their recent inflow of immigrants with increased diversity will affect their socialist ideals.

Add to that list Ireland, New Zealand, and Belgium, also with around 10 million or less people, and the Netherlands with 17 million. Even Canada has a smaller population than California. Thus, all of these examples are the application of the socialist model to small countries. With the exception of Canada, all of these countries have traditionally had less diversity than the United States and had closely-knit societies.

To round out the top ten socialist meccas, we have France with 65 million people and unemployment that has been hovering around 10% for some time. That's not exactly an endorsement of socialism. Recently, the French are showing signs of dissatisfaction with their socialist experiment that began in the 1980s. Other socialist countries show lower unemployment figures by hiding the statistics and reclassifying non-working people on welfare as not being in the workforce.

What works in a homogeneous nation of 5 to 10 million will not necessarily work in a diverse nation of 320 million with many internal divisions.

We even have hints at a form of socialism in the United States with the entire medical industry controlled by Medicare and a handful of medical insurance companies. The result? Medical costs take a substantial and growing share of the U.S. economy. Socialists would point out that our medical costs are higher than in socialist countries, but with all of their subsidized costs, it's hard to make a fair comparison.

Probably the biggest flaw in the socialist model has to do with taxation as discussed in the section on Taxes. Tax rates above 40% do not appear to increase tax revenues proportionately or sometimes at all. Increasing rates above this level changes taxpayer behavior in terms of avoidance and changes the nature of investing away from job creation.

Furthermore, while Sweden, as an example, has a more equal distribution of wealth than in the United States, they do this with a top income tax rate of 56% and GDP per capita (using purchasing power parity) that is 20% below that of the United States. In other words, they achieve equality by lowering incomes.

Let's look at this comparison another way. Start with the United States today and have all of the one-percenters leave the country with their income and wealth. Assume that doesn't disrupt the economy in any negative way except subtracting their numbers. Then redistribute the remaining income from the middle class to the poor. The result would be Sweden on a per capita basis with the middle class taking lower incomes to support the poor. That is the inconvenient truth that the socialists don't tell you, one of the unfortunate side-effects.

In a truly socialist world, anyone who earns more than $16,400 per year (worldwide average income) would need to give their excess income to the poor in third-world countries. If you're not willing to do so, you should ask yourself what the morality is of expecting wealth redistribution in your country, and not doing your part by sending your excess earnings to third-world countries. Indeed, if we open our borders to unlimited immigration, we are making the choice to share our income and wealth with the world. In fact, outsourcing 3.2 million jobs to China supports the socialist ideal of redistributing income from the rich (Americans) to the poor (Chinese).

Despite what some people would have you believe, socialism was not the engine that turned the United States into the world's greatest economy. That award goes to entrepreneurship. It goes to those who ventured into the unknown and built small and new businesses. In fact, China became the number two economy in the world when they moved away from socialism and toward entrepreneurship, which, by the way, was native to China long before it became popular in the West.

Russia, however, has failed to grow her economy; instead, they replaced the central planning of socialism with the central planning of an oligopoly, which operates like a medieval feudal fiefdom.

CAPITALISM & ENTREPRENEURIALISM

Doesn't capitalism lead to crony capitalism?

Adam Smith is thought of as the father of capitalism, despite the fact that "capitalism" doesn't appear in his book *Wealth of Nations*, which was published in 1776. Capitalism or the private ownership of property existed long before Adam Smith. His great achievement was his exploration of free markets, competition, and about how the "invisible hand" guides markets. By the way, the "invisible hand" is nothing more than human nature applied across large populations. It's a study in human behavior, not some mythical gobbledygook.

Smith recognized the power of private ownership to incentivize people to innovate and produce better products and services at more affordable prices that benefit all of the people. Who among us are not angered by higher prices and shortages, and thrilled by lower prices and wider selection of goods and services?

He also warned that the biggest enemy of free markets was monopolies and, by extension, oligopolies that harkened back to feudalism with a select few controlling the wealth and the means of production. "The price of monopoly is upon every occasion the highest which can be got," Adam Smith said. "The natural price, or the price of free competition, on the contrary, is the lowest which can be taken, not upon every occasion indeed, but for any considerable time." Thus, competitive capitalism leads to lower prices and greater selection.

Adam Smith was warning about the anti-competitive implications of monopolies and oligopolies that distort the free market and destroy competition. They do this by withholding supply and manipulating prices and wages to maximize profits in ways they couldn't in a free economy. He was warning about the British mercantile trade system that restricted competition by awarding trade monopolies. He talked about how the inefficiencies of the mercantile monopolies were expensive for Britain as the mother country.

Capitalism has gotten a bad rap because those who dislike it equate capitalism with monopolies and oligopolies, but monopolies and oligopolies are not capitalism. They are the enemies of capitalism.

Monopolies are not the free enterprise system that Adam Smith championed. He championed the entrepreneurial spirit of competition where individuals who create better products and services at competitive prices succeed. This entrepreneurship is what built America from a sparsely populated wilderness into a world power in less than a hundred years. In fact, this is exactly how Apple and Microsoft became successful before they became so large.

The true value of capitalism and free enterprise is to enjoy the incentives and benefits when you produce better products and services and do so at lower prices over time, both of which benefit the people. Monopolies and oligopolies destroy the incentive to improve products and reduce prices since they hold the power to keep prices up and wages down. They lack the incentive to make improvements; thus they do not represent free enterprise. We can see this in the number of entrepreneurial companies bought by megaliths who can't create such entrepreneurial innovation on their own.

Perhaps it would be best to think of the free enterprise system as a pendulum. When it swings toward too little regulation, monopolies and oligopolies rise to consolidate their grip on markets so they can control supplies, lower wages, and increase prices. As it swings toward too much regulation, as it has in certain cases today, the incentives for small businesses disappear. Those businesses then either close or sell to big conglomerates, leading toward ever more powerful oligopolies.

The system needs to balance between providing enough

rewards for the success of individuals and small businesses while preventing the few from growing so large they eliminate competition. When the oil trusts got too big in the early twentieth century, Teddy Roosevelt broke them up. At other times over the past hundred years, the government has stepped in from an antitrust standpoint to prevent the consolidation of industries into what threatened to become monopolies and oligopolies.

Today, we face unprecedented consolidation in banking, healthcare, and other industries. In part this is a response to increased government regulations and complexity in which government brings in the very big companies to write the regulations that then benefit these companies over smaller businesses that are not represented.

The biggest consolidation risk has been in banking, but another that threatens to affect every American is the consolidation taking place in the healthcare industry as drug companies and healthcare providers consolidate in order to deal with what is becoming an oligopoly of health insurance companies and Medicare and complex regulations beyond the capability of small healthcare providers to understand, let alone comply with. Included in this consolidation are recent mergers among pharmacies. Bigger is not better.

In attempting to manage the economy, the government becomes bigger to deal with big companies. Companies consolidate and become bigger to deal with big government. There becomes an unholy alliance between big government, big corporations, and big unions that squeeze out smaller entrepreneurial companies that are the true engines of economic growth. With this trend toward big companies and away from small entrepreneurial businesses, it should come as no surprise that we have had slow job growth over the past 15 years.

It's far easier for government bureaucrats to deal with a few big players in the economy rather than millions of small businesses. Thus big government tends to favor big corporations. Complex regulations are often written with the help of big corporations as was the ACA health plan, but bigness destroys incentives.

Monopolies and oligopolies are not capitalism or free enterprise. They are corporate feudalism. Free enterprise is about small businesses that today are being strangled by massive government regulation intended to regulate huge companies. Only by limiting the consolidation of industry after industry can we preserve the competition that has allowed the free enterprise system to improve the lives of all Americans. Instead, we have allowed mergers to continue until we have banks too big to fail and industries with limited competition.

We need to dust off our antitrust laws to make sure that mergers do not diminish the vital competitiveness of our economy, and examine all government regulations that penalize small businesses in the name of controlling big ones.

Political mantras will not fix this. Neither will left-right politics. Free enterprise is the core of America's promise and success, but it will only thrive by balancing the incentives to succeed with restraints on monopolies and oligopolies.

INTERNATIONAL TRADE

China has reportedly acquired 3.2 million American jobs as a result of globalization. For this alone, why shouldn't we block trade agreements, including the Trans-Pacific Partnership?

Those who rail against international trade agreements and free trade might want to reflect on the mercantile system from a hundred years ago. In that system, the mother countries (England, France, and Holland) had trading relationships with their colonies and limited trade with other European countries and their colonies. In other words, it consisted of monopolies and oligopolies.

Those systems had one purpose, to suck value from the colonies to benefit the home country. Employment in the colonies was based on low wages and a monopoly arrangement in which the colonies were not allowed to trade to their favor, only with their mother country. This was one of the irritations that led to the American Revolution. It was also one of the fundamental structures of the colonial experience.

You might also want to reflect on a major contributing factor to the Great Depression of the 1930s. The stock market bubble hit its peak in 1926. The market fell and recovered to that peak again in 1929. While the stock-market bubble looked like the housing collapse in 2007, it had one additional event going for it—Smoot-Hawley.

The Smoot-Hawley Bill was a restrictive trade action that significantly increased tariffs on imports. It passed the House of Representatives in May 1929. By September of that year, many of

America's trading partners were threatening retaliation if the bill became law, which it did in 1930. The threat of a trade war shocked the markets, sending them into a tailspin. A trade war followed that cut U.S. exports by 65%, took away millions of American jobs, and directly contributed at least 1.5% to the economic collapse. The indirect side-effect was much larger.

The United States, which had been excluded from the restrictive European mercantile system that existed prior to World War I, was the main driver toward creating the free trade arrangements after World War II that have continued through today. America benefitted from freer trade than what existed in either the mercantile system or the trade wars of the 1930s. For the most part, trade has replaced military conflict in Europe and East Asia.

Those who point to job losses after a trade deal look at only part of what is happening, though it is the most visible part. The other side of a "good" deal involves increased exports in other industries, which bring overall job growth. The newer jobs are harder to identify, which is why we focus on the jobs lost.

Think of it this way. Each of us trades our labor for goods and services we want. Very few of us produce all of our food and other goods and services. We trade because it's better for us to do our specific jobs and buy goods and services from others who specialize at what they do. If we had to produce everything for ourselves, we might be self-sufficient, but our standard of living would be much lower as it was 100 years ago when most Americans still lived on farms and rural communities. Imagine how you would make a car or even a cell-phone network on your own.

Still, not all trade deals are good.

Lowering tariffs with a friendly nation who does the same for us can allow trade where each nation can focus on what they do best and thereby benefit both countries. A deal with a country that takes advantage of American generosity by manipulating prices to benefit their workers is not a good deal.

The test of a good deal is how it affects our overall trade balances over time, not our trade with an individual country. If we run a trade deficit with Mexico, yet make it up with surpluses elsewhere so our overall trade over time is balanced, the deficit with Mexico isn't a problem.

Unfortunately, the U.S. has run heavy overall trade losses for a very long time with both Mexico and China, leading to a significant amount of U.S. wealth being held by foreigners. Part of America's lingering trade deficits has been our continued dependence on foreign oil, which we could have done more about over the past 40 years. Part is that we've allowed nations like China and Mexico to run heavy surpluses against us without having other places to offset these deficits.

What options do we have?

1. We could reject the Trans-Pacific Partnership (which includes Mexico but not China). That would likely bring few if any jobs back to America. It might slow the transfer of jobs to Mexico, but there are other agreements in place with Mexico if this doesn't pass. Keeping the agreement would strengthen nations on the Pacific Rim as a counterweight to Chinese expansion. Perhaps we should demand some transparency and revisit some of the provisions. One provision allows foreign corporations to bypass domestic courts. Another is the patent and intellectual property provisions. Still, walking away from this agreement altogether will strengthen China's position in the western Pacific.
2. We could renegotiate our agreements with China as long as we recognize that the United States is no longer the 800 pound gorilla. We need to deal with China as an equal partner, which means we have to bring more than just demands and threats to the table in order to negotiate. At the same time, we need to address intellectual property and currency issues, while recognizing that anything that smacks of a trade war will threaten to kill American export jobs and hurt our overall economy.
3. If the United States (as discussed elsewhere) adopted a Value Added Tax (VAT) in place of certain other taxes, it would go a long way toward leveling the playing field with our trade partners who use this method of taxation. Properly set up, it would make our exports more competitive. It would make imports more expensive, which would favor bringing manufacturing jobs back to America. In addition, since most of our trading partners

already use VAT, it shouldn't start a trade war like applying tariffs or cancelling trade agreements. The real question is why neither party is in favor of considering this option.

As we approach our trade deals, it behooves us to bear in mind that restricting trade comes with serious side-effects to American workers. Those who receive jobs as a result of cutting trade might feel grateful, but a big consequence of blocking trade will be higher prices that will hurt all Americans, and in particular the working poor. Furthermore, trade cuts both ways. If we restrict imports, other nations will restrict our exports and those American jobs will go away, as happened in the 1930s.

Where are the American jobs that will go away in a trade war? Look at where the United States has significant exports:

- Machines, engines, and pumps
- Transportation equipment
- Chemicals
- Electronic equipment
- Aircraft and spacecraft
- Vehicles
- Oil
- Medical and technical equipment
- Plastics
- Pharmaceuticals

If you work in one of these industries and we enter into a trade war, you could see your job disappear. Nevertheless, we should examine why we continue to run trade deficits and seek ways to fix the problem.

Perhaps it's time that we consider implementing a Value Added Tax (VAT). If this were done on a revenue neutral basis by reducing business income tax rates, then this would make it more lucrative for American businesses to sell abroad and to bring jobs to the United States. Both effects would increase American jobs, a win-win scenario.

BIG LEGAL AWARDS

Big settlements in the legal tort system exist to punish corporations and hold them accountable, right?

Maybe that's the intent, but that's not how it works.

Slick lawyers have found a loophole in the legal system and turned it into a gold mine. They've figured out how to milk the system and make big money for themselves (their fees) as they sue mega-corporations and healthcare providers (with their mega-corporation malpractice insurance) to obtain tort judgments for their clients. They play upon the rage we feel when presented with the little guy who has sustained a loss while this deep pocket stands nearby.

I'm not against anyone getting their day in court, but what are the side-effects of the supersized awards with punitive damages intended to punish corporations? These awards go beyond reasonable costs to the injured party and include awards in class action suits that mainly benefit the attorneys.

In the latter, an attorney obtains a judgment against an insurance company or a phone company for "taking advantage" of its customers. Ten million people get $10 each to cover their damages for a total of $100 million. Meanwhile, the attorneys walk away with $50 million. Who benefits from this action? The attorneys get rich while customers and policyholders barely get enough for pizza and drinks.

Still, we made that nasty corporation pay, right? Back to that in a minute.

Let's take the case of medical malpractice. A patient goes into the hospital with a set of symptoms. The doctors try to address those symptoms, but the patient suffers a loss. Perhaps her leg has to be amputated. The patient has indeed suffered and will need a prosthetic, physical therapy, and will have to deal with emotional distress. Who can put a price on that?

Since she doesn't have the money to deal with all of the costs associated with her loss, a lawyer tells her to sue the hospital and the doctor. The lawyer is only being an altruistic good citizen with nothing personal to gain. Right!

So, they sue.

The hospital settles since they don't want the bad publicity, despite how they followed protocol for the set of symptoms they found. During their investigation, the hospital administration learns that the hospital failed to perform a test that could have found the underlying symptoms, if only they had reason to perform that test.

Afterwards, it's easy to second guess, but the woman needs money, the hospital has money, so the lawyer says, "Let's sue."

What happens?

The woman gets $20 million. She's not happy, though the money goes a long way toward helping her with recovery. Justice is served. The lawyer banks another $10 million, which makes him a top one-one-hundredth-of-one-percenter (0.01%) just based on this one win. The hospital gets punished for following protocol and forks out $30 million.

That's not the end.

The hospital's malpractice insurance company pays out the $30 million. The insurance company raises premiums to this hospital and to all hospital and medical practices in the area to cover having to pay this award. The healthcare providers then have to pass on the added insurance premium costs to consumers. That means increasing prices to everyone. The hospital suffers some loss in prestige, but no loss in income. Doctors and hospital staff go about their business without experiencing any loss except for the hospital administration second-guessing their medical practices.

Ultimately, it's future patients who pay the $30 million as part of higher healthcare costs. Perhaps that gets pushed on their medical insurance companies who increase healthcare premiums to cover their costs. Bottom line: the intended target (the hospital and doctors) are not suffering from the tort settlement.

We're still not done.

Based on having to settle and pass through the cost of higher malpractice premiums, the hospital and doctors change their protocols to perform more tests that are not needed for 99% of their patients. The additional tests and procedures increase the medical costs that insurance companies have to pay. That ensures that healthcare costs continue to grow faster than the economy. The hospitals make more money on the increased procedures. The medical supply companies make more money selling equipment and supplies for the tests. The threat of lawsuit weighs more heavily in their decisions than the additional unnecessary tests they're doing.

To cover higher costs related to the additional tests and procedures, healthcare insurance companies increase premiums that have to be paid by people who have individual healthcare insurance and by businesses that now have a higher cost of hiring employees. Those businesses at some point will make the decision to automate or outsource since they can't afford the cost of wages, taxes, and escalating medical costs. They might even drop medical coverage for their employees, if they can, leaving their employees to pay the exorbitant healthcare premiums themselves.

Who actually pays for the woman's $20 million award and the $10 million pocketed by the altruistic attorney? That would be consumers and employees. Furthermore, because of the additional tests that healthcare providers now perform, the cost to consumers is far in excess of the $30 million award.

If you are a beneficiary of one of these lawsuits, recovering actual costs, then this becomes a matter of society helping you get your life back together. On the other hand, if you are the beneficiary of a bonus win above actual costs, you should thank all those millions of ordinary Americans who made it possible and will ultimately pay for it, despite the fact that they had nothing to do with your injury or loss. Punitive awards turn out to be nothing more than a wealth transfer from ordinary Americans—a lottery win those people didn't know they paid for.

Those altruistic attorneys will cry foul, but is their anger a result of their good will toward their clients or their potential financial loss if this loophole gets closed? Remember, these are one-percenter attorneys. And we're talking about punitive damages and oversized awards.

Here's the problem with the "sock-it-to-the-corporation" mantra floated by these attorneys and their supporters. Who is a corporation? You may have touched a building owned by a corporation, talked to employees of that corporation, even received a check from a corporation, but have you ever seen or touched a corporation?

A corporation first and foremost is a fiction, yet a useful tool for organizing people. It's the recognition by the government of a group of people working together as having a group legal identity. It's a collection of people, most of whom are anonymous to customers. Yet corporations serve very useful purposes. First, they allow a group of people to work together on complex products and services, such as telephone networks, building cars and airplanes, and running hospitals. Second, they survive the owners, which allows the product and service to continue and for employment to go on after the owners' death.

When a corporation (hospital, insurance company, etc.) pays out a tort settlement, the money gets paid by the corporation, but who really pays? Some one-percenter, right?

If you were in charge of some corporation that had to pay out $30 million, would you take it out of your own pocket? Unlikely. You would have insurance pay and then figure out how to cover the increase in insurance premiums by raising prices, if you can, or reducing costs. In the case of hospitals, increasing prices will indirectly hurt consumers as healthcare costs rise. Cutting costs will mean fewer jobs either at the hospital or with their suppliers.

Let's say, for the sake of argument, that the corporation can't raise prices or reduce costs either due to government regulation or market pressures. Then what happens?

The corporation's income drops. This hurts the corporation's stock price, which hurts wealthy owners and anyone who has a pension or a 401k. In other words, the pain gets spread around to more than just the wealthy. In addition, if the pain is severe enough, the hospital may have to close its doors as hundreds have over the past 10 years.

Ultimately, the woman who received the $20 million will pay for part of her own award and that of others who have benefitted from tort lawyers. Meanwhile, the tort attorneys become wealthy enough to have their own conventions and lobbyists to keep the system as it is.

They are some of the wealthiest contributors to candidates in both parties to maintain the status quo. Despite the fact that being a tort attorney can be quite lucrative, it's interesting that competition has not brought down their fees. It makes you wonder.

The next time you're called on as a juror or as a complainant in one of these lawsuits, consider that the lawyer has a significant financial interest in a big settlement that most likely will be paid by ordinary citizens who carried no blame for the suit. That is the inconvenient truth of the tort system.

CONFLICT OF INTEREST

Why do we tolerate conflicts of interest?

Many years ago, while working for a public utility, we had to address the perceived conflict of interest in which the public service commission approved rate hikes from the utility in exchange for the utility's support. I was too low in the company to know the particulars or even if they were true, but it was perceived that there was an unhealthy arrangement that appeared as a conflict of interest.

We now face a different conflict of interest. In this one, individuals pay fees to a group that uses those fees to make donations to public officials. Those public officials increase benefits to the members of this group who then pay more fees to the group bosses to make more donations to public officials. It's a feedback loop that has afflicted most states and cities to the point of potential bankruptcy, and yet it continues.

The winners in this game have been the public officials who have enjoyed power and the perks of offices paid for by the bosses who hold a monopoly in the collection of fees. Winners have also included the groups' bosses who have enjoyed great success in providing benefits to their members and power to themselves. The members themselves have enjoyed better wages and benefits.

What's not to like?

The unfortunate side-effect is that ordinary citizen taxpayers have no say in the matter, yet they are expected to pay for this arrangement with higher taxes. That's not even the best part. The group bosses get the public officials to make legally-binding promises to the members, while making no provisions to pay for those commitments. These are future benefits, pension benefits, guaranteed by laws enacted by the public officials who benefitted from this arrangement. They have even made it illegal to discharge these benefits in a bankruptcy. In other words, they have legally committed the taxpayers of each community to pay ever higher taxes to pay for this scheme.

Bottom line: taxpayers are forced to pay higher taxes that go to the members who are forced to pay membership fees that line the pockets of the bosses and the public officials. This is a clear conflict of interest that shows no sign of ending.

By not paying enough into a pension benefits trust fund, the public officials avoid having to face up to the cost of the promises they're making in exchange for campaign donations. They keep kicking the can down the road, hoping they'll retire before the bills come due.

We're talking about public service unions. There was no fair negotiation for the wage and benefit increases they obtained, just a cozy back-room deal that mainly benefitted the bosses and the politicians they supported.

The case for public service unions is that their members are at the mercy of governmental procedures that leave them at a disadvantage relative to asserting their rights. The individual employee stands no chance in negotiating pay, benefits or grievances against big government.

Even FDR, the champion of worker rights, cautioned us about the conflict of interest inherent in public service unions.

Public service unions make campaign contributions to state politicians in exchange for favorable laws pertaining to recruiting new members (all members of a class are automatically enrolled), collecting dues (mandatory), and obtaining pay increases, pension benefits, and other benefits from the state through those politicians.

In exchange for campaign support by the union bosses, those politicians pass laws benefitting the public service unions with no oversight by the taxpayers who have to pay the bills. The biggest abuse has been in public service pensions, where the unfunded benefits are kicked down the road, but the benefit to those politicians and union bosses are immediate.

Meanwhile, citizens are expected to pay whatever taxes are necessary to cover the cozy relationship between these politicians and their union boss friends, because those politicians have written it into law. In fact, it's taxpayer money that is filling the pockets of union bosses and the politicians who have created this conflict of interest.

The question is who in this process represents the people who have to pay taxes?

Public service employees deserve to be paid fairly for their work, but as states face the prospects of bankruptcy over these conflict of interest arrangements, one or both of two groups will have to pay.

If the unfunded pension benefits promised by public officials are cut back to what the states can afford to pay, to what people working in other industries would be entitled to, then the workers who have built their lives around these promises stand to be devastated, particularly those near or in retirement.

If the workers don't take the cuts, then taxes will have to be increased significantly to pay for these future promises, promises that taxpayers were never allowed to vote on. The real tragedy is that the union bosses and the politicians who brought this about aren't being asked to chip in. They are not even being held accountable.

This represents a Ponzi scheme with the taxpayers and public service employees holding the bag. The problem isn't so much the wages, current benefits, and other negotiating protection these workers get. It's the pension and other future benefits that are hidden from voters, promises that future voters are committed to.

WALL STREET REFORM

What will it take to prevent another Wall Street meltdown?

The Wall Street banks, big insurance, and investment banks in concert with Fannie Mae and Freddie Mac orchestrated a real estate bubble that burst in 2007 sending the U.S. economy into a tailspin. Yet, none of the officials running those organizations were prosecuted or made to pay the price for their role in the crash. Today, the too-big-to-fail banks are even larger and more concentrated than they were prior to the crash thanks to mergers sanctioned by the government.

The federal government played a significant role in the crash. In the late 1990s, they removed the Glass-Steagall Act, which previously prevented commercial banks from engaging in risky investment banking and insurance activities. After 9/11, Fannie Mae and Freddie Mac, as instruments of the government, promoted home-ownership by buying and insuring questionable loans. When the real estate bubble burst, they couldn't cover their loan obligations.

The focus of many people has been on Wall Street vs. Main Street, but it isn't that simple, since the government was also involved. Yet, most of us agree that the circumstances leading up to the 2007-9 crash were unacceptable. What can we do about it?

1. Prevent Fannie Mae and Freddie Mac from buying and insuring loans they don't understand. This will remove incentives for shady mortgage lenders to package bad deals and pass them along. Make it a punishable crime for

executives at Fannie Mae and Freddie Mac to buy or insure loans they haven't inspected and set standards that would prevent future complicity in bad loans.

2. When a company needs to be bailed out, allow the government to claw back any bonuses that company paid in the previous 12-24 months to help pay for the bailout. After all, why should the company's executives get to keep the bonuses they earned in the build-up to collapse? This will put executives on notice to prevent their companies from needing a bailout. Spreading the pain will incentivize better decisions to prevent future disasters.
3. Glass-Steagall itself would not have prevented the 2007-08 collapse but its principles would have helped. We could institute some form of Glass-Steagall to prevent commercial banks from getting involved in risky investments and apply similar guidelines to large investment banks (like Lehman Brothers) and big insurance companies (like AIG). To avoid more banking consolidations, we should make sure the guidelines do not penalize smaller companies, particularly those who didn't collapse. An unfortunate side-effect of current regulations to prevent too-big-to-fail is that they punish small banks, and encourage more consolidations in the industry and more too-big-to-fail.
4. As part of dealing with collapsing banks during and after 2007-08, the government encouraged or at least approved the merger of weak banks into stronger banks, creating even bigger banks. Perhaps we should apply anti-trust regulations to the too-big-to-fail banks. If you're too big and need bailing out, perhaps you don't deserve to be so big. If banks don't like the anti-trust approach, then they should have found a way to avoid the collapse in the first place.
5. Modify Dodd-Frank so that it doesn't penalize smaller banks for the actions of the too-big-to-fail banks. The number of commercial banks has dropped from 14,400 in 1984 to 5,381 in 2015. This consolidation has contributed to too-big-to-fail. Additional regulations as part of Dodd-Frank seem to have the side-effect of continuing this consolidation, with 1,838 more closures since the collapse.

The consolidation of too-big-to-fail banks continues. Since the crash, JPMorgan Chase has acquired Washington Mutual and Bear Stearns. Wells Fargo has acquired Wachovia. Bank of America has merged with Merrill Lynch and Countrywide Financial. We should do more to encourage smaller community banks instead of building a regulator structure that favors the rich.

6. Here's a thought on bailing out the banks. In future, bail out the depositors and break up the banks that fail. FDIC insurance is all about protecting depositors. Let the banks reorganize under better management that won't make such risky investments.
7. If there are individuals who knowingly packaged bad loans as part of the housing bubble, bring them to justice.

If we want to prevent the next crisis with too-big-to-fail, then let's stop promoting the consolidation of the financial industry with regulations that penalize the smaller community banks for the actions of the already too-big-to-fail. After all, big banks benefit by the closure of more community banks.

CAMPAIGN FINANCE

Big money controls political campaign financing. What can we do about it?

Political campaigns in the U.S. have gotten out of control. It now takes two years and billions of dollars to run a presidential campaign. In the parliamentary system of various other Western countries, a campaign for leadership may last 6-8 weeks at a small fraction of the cost.

Special interests with deep pockets throw their money around to keep their loopholes at the expense of the American people. They are organized, well financed, and at a time when it takes billions to run for president, they wield power disproportionate to their numbers or their value to American society. Their collective interest perverts the political process.

One example, as discussed under Big Legal Awards, is that large tort settlements penalize ordinary Americans more than the intended targets. Another example is corn-ethanol. It's not as "green" as advertised. It benefits a small group of people, but the first political test of a presidential campaign is in Iowa, which is heavily into corn-ethanol.

Then there are the big banks, oil companies, and the list goes on. We are losing the country to special interests.

We live in the Internet age with democratization of information; some would say too much information. Why not keep the debates as an opportunity for candidates to differentiate themselves within their parties and have the rest of their campaigns run through their campaign websites? Individuals could contribute directly through online payment systems like PayPal or by check sent to their candidate of choice.

With that as a first step, how can we do away with the buying of the presidency? Eliminate all concentrated big money spent on campaigns:

1. Super-PACs on all sides.
2. Corporate spending on elections. Employees can make their own contributions.
3. Union spending on elections. Union members can make their own contributions.
4. Foundation and other organization spending on elections.

In other words, get rid of all group spending and make this all about the individual voter. That would eliminate the consolidation of power into the hands of the bosses. Instead of letting the powerful make the decisions, it would return power to the people and let individuals make their own decisions of who to support and give their donations to.

In addition to the debates, the parties could set up Internet campaign forums that would allow each candidate trying for the party's leadership to pitch in his/her own words as to why we should vote for them. Candidates could pitch people to visit their campaign website to learn more and contribute.

We live in the Internet age. Why not ban all of the wealthy (PAC, corporate, union, foundation) donations and use the Internet to bring candidates and citizens together without the Super-PAC/corporate/union interference?

It's a pipe dream since anyone with a blog or social media account can use free speech to promote the candidate of their choice. Making these changes would shift the power from wealthy groups to celebrities, who would use their social media clout to back the candidates of their choice. In other words, we would be shifting from one group with too much influence for their numbers to another.

INVESTING IN JOBS

During the 1960s, the government's investment in the Moon mission spurred innovation and economic activity during that decade. Other investments have been made over the years, including in the Internet.

Recently, one candidate proposed spending $1 trillion dollars over five years to create 13 million jobs through rebuilding roads, bridges, and other infrastructure that need repair. When you deal with large enough numbers, anything sounds possible. After all, $1 trillion dollars (that's 12 zeros) ought to buy a lot of benefits.

The question is: who would want the jobs this candidate is proposing?

Simple math: Divide $1 trillion by 5 years and by 13 million Americans. That equals $15,385 per year. Divide that by 2080 work hours a year (52 weeks times 40 hours) and you get $7.40/hour.

Investment in jobs	$1,000,000,000,000
Divide by 5 years	200,000,000,000
Americans getting jobs	13,000,000
Annual income/person	15,385
Annual work hours	2,080
Hourly wage	7.40

Thus, this candidate wants to create 13 million jobs that pay less than half of the minimum wage he proposes.

It sounds as if this proposal will grow to $2 trillion. That money will have to come from somewhere. You're probably thinking the one-percenters, but $2 trillion of additional taxes over 5 years applied to the one-percenters would add 23% of additional income tax on top of their current 27% tax for a 50% tax rate, plus whatever they will be asked to pay for additional Medicare coverage and other costs.

Under the section on Taxes, we've already explored how increasing tax rates to this level will not increase tax revenues by equal amounts. At some point, the cost of these programs will trickle down to higher taxes and costs for the middle class.

Is this a proposal about creating jobs or buying votes?

MYTH OF ECONOMIC GROWTH

You just heard that the economy grew 2.4% last year, isn't that great?

With population growth around 0.8%, that represents 1.6% real growth per person. That's good, isn't it?

Let's say you buy some fresh fruits and vegetables because you know they're good for you. By the time you get around to eating them, they've gone bad. You throw them out and buy microwave foods that are easier to prepare and don't spoil as fast. Your food bill has gone up on account of replacing the wasted food. You save a little less and vow not to do it again.

Bless you. You have just boosted the U.S. economy.

By buying more food than you ate, your purchases allowed the store to sell more to you and in turn buy more from the farmers. More people are employed due to your generous act, but are you any better off? No, you've just done a wealth transfer from you to people you will probably never meet.

In another situation, let's say that today you stay home to raise your child. You don't earn a cent and you don't pay for childcare. To that extent, even though you work hard, you are not participating in the U.S. economy, though you are when you buy food and supplies.

Money is tight and there are repairs to make, so you decide to do something about it. You find a job paying $30,000 a year. You find a childcare provider who watches several children and you pay them $12,000 per year. You pay for clothes for work, lunches for work days, and transportation for a total of $5,000 a year. You also pay for things you couldn't have afforded before, like replacing your old car and the leaky water heater. At the end of the day, you've spent every cent you earned, but your car works fine and your water heater doesn't leak.

New job	$ 30,000
Childcare	(12,000)
Work related costs	(5,000)
Discretionary income	13,000

You have entered the economy. Your wages may or may not come from a new job, but your childcare and other costs are a direct and immediate boost to the economy. Bless you.

The economy has grown $30,000 in response to your additional spending. The question is do you feel $30,000 a year wealthier since you're working, $13,000 better off which is the amount you clear after childcare and job related costs or something else. In effect, while the economy has grown $30,000, you only have $13,000 more to spend on non-work related costs than you did before.

Indeed, if each of us were self-sufficient, growing all of our own food and other needs, the economy would grind to zero, even though people would have food to eat, clothes to wear, and a roof over their heads.

The point is that economic reports do not tell the whole story. Sometimes, we, as individuals, outsource what we used to do for ourselves, like childcare. At other times, we decide to do more for ourselves like doing our own home repairs when times are tough. Other than having to do more or less ourselves, the quality of our lives does not go up and down by the amount that we spend. Thus, reported economic growth doesn't tell the full story.

PART 7: IMMIGRATION

≈≈≈≈≈≈≈≈≈≈≈≈≈≈≈≈≈≈≈≈≈≈≈≈≈≈≈

IMMIGRATION HISTORY

What does history tell us about immigration?

Yes, this country was built by immigrants and descendants of immigrants. Nonetheless, over most of the past 150 years, immigration has been more restricted than today and quite restrictive during 1930-45, when the economy was struggling and then when we were at war. The only other time that immigration was as high as it has been during 1989-2013 was during a rapidly growing economy before World War I, and that only lasted 10 years. The current rapid pace of immigration has been going on for 25 years.

	Average Legal Immigration (000's)
1865-1904	408
1905-1914	1012
1915-1930	357
1930-1945	47
1946-1988	366
1989-2013	1012

<See Bibliography source 16>

Those who don't see a problem with open immigration should talk to the Native Americans about how well that worked out for them. First, a few European immigrants arrived. They traded and shared with the Native Americans. More immigrants came. They became strong and pushed Native Americans out of their lands. The few who survived were pushed onto reservations. In retrospect, perhaps Native Americans should have been more proactive about dealing with their immigration problem.

We could jump back 10,000 years and ask what happened to the Clovis Man or whoever else was living in the Americas at the time the Native Americans arrived and took over. Those people have lost their voice.

Immigration has not just been an issue in America, however.

Talk to the Britons about immigration. No, not the Celtic Irish, Welsh, and Scots. They arrived in the centuries before the Romans. Think of the other Britons, the ones who built Stonehenge and other monuments. They had a society on the islands long before the Celts arrived. Where are their descendants? They were either absorbed into Celtic society or died off, to become a footnote to archeological history. Perhaps they should have paid more attention to immigration.

Some fifteen centuries ago, Celtic Britain had an immigration problem after the Romans left. Angles and Saxons decided to settle there. Certain Celtic tribes fighting among themselves even invited Angles, Saxons, and Danes to help in their fights against their neighbors. The outsiders decided they liked the land. They immigrated to Britain and took over.

Long ago, the Indo-Europeans arrived on the Indian subcontinent as immigrants and conquerors. They took over, using a caste system over the more populous natives so that the newcomers could retain control.

Talk to the large Syrian Christian communities in the 7th century when Muslim armies swept in and at the point of a sword forced families to submit to Islam or die. Ask them how well immigration went for them.

Now, Europe is inviting millions of new immigrants who will bring existential changes to European culture. Talk to citizens of Paris, Brussels, Cologne, and Sweden about how well immigration is going for them. Citizens are being told they have to adapt to the newcomers instead of the other way around.

Why?

The newcomers arrived because they believed Europe was better than what they left. Now they want to change Europe into what they came from. That makes no sense.

You don't have to be anti-immigrant, racist or any of a number of other labels that pro-immigration advocates throw out in order to see that uncontrolled immigration is a problem. Whether the problems get resolved and whether the changes brought by the immigrants turn out to be good or bad remains to be seen. In either case, being concerned about the level of immigration doesn't equate to a lack of compassion for the people involved.

If we do not learn from history, we will fall victim to the same mistakes of the past. As described in the section on Depressed Wages, low levels of immigration aren't a problem. High levels have been associated with depressed wages. The immigration-deniers, who put their collective heads in the sand, are not helping to resolve the issues. In fact, their actions are directly hurting the poor, not only citizens, but also new arrivals, who can expect lower pay as a result of high immigration.

The history of migrations has been that they have brought great cultural diversity to the lands where they settled. They brought new technologies and ideas, often with respect to warfare and religion. They also brought tremendous cultural change. Still, immigration did not always benefit the native culture they settled among.

When populations were low, as they were in America over 100 years ago, immigration played a significant role in the growth of the country. Today, with all due respect to the Native Americans, there are no lands that are declared open for settling.

Perhaps it's time to be more selective with immigration. Some immigration is good for the growth of the nation. Too much, creates not only diversity, but division and depressed wages, which weakens the country. In addition, bringing in immigrants faster than the economy and our society can absorb them will stir up disappointment and anger, rather than gratitude for being given a new home, particularly when it's associated with low wages and unemployment.

That will lead to social unrest.

So, embrace the immigrants, but let's make this a win for them and for those who came before by slowing down until the economy can catch up. We've had depressed wages for too long already.

IMMIGRATION & DIVERSITY

Like the United States, Rome embraced diversity almost from its beginning. They brought citizenship to the Etruscans, the Celtic peoples, even to Germanic tribes. Somewhere along the way, Rome lost its unifying values. They tried to compensate by making Christianity the state religion in the 4th Century. They even split into the Western Empire and in the east what became the Byzantine Empire in order to better manage their diverse culture.

Not long after the split, the Western Empire fell to Germanic invasions. In part, this was because Rome had made promises to the Goths and other immigrants, allowing them to settle on Roman lands. When Rome was unable to fulfill her promises, the Goths sacked Rome in 410 AD and things went downhill after that.

The United States also risks broken promises if we bring immigrants in too fast and they face depressed wages and limited opportunities.

The Byzantine Empire lasted another 1,000 years after Rome fell, though during much of the last half of its existence, it consisted primarily of western Turkey, Greece, and the nearby Balkans. Toward the end, it had been reduced to the city-state of Constantinople. Rome's experiment with diversity lasted a long time, but in the end, Rome fell in part because promises made to immigrants could not be kept.

Talk to the Romans about their experience with immigration from the Goths, the Huns, and the Vandals. That's right, Rome fell.

That's not to speak against diversity or multiculturalism. I was multicultural before most Americans alive today understood what that meant. Unfortunately, when diversity leads to a loss of unifying core values, without replacing those with new values, the society begins to spin apart.

That has not been a problem facing Japan, China, Denmark, Sweden, and Norway in the past. It will be interesting to see how the Scandinavian countries deal with the increased levels of diversity that they have recently embraced. Will that enhance or complicate their social and economic models?

Diversity and the blending of new cultures have indeed made America stronger. It's interesting to note that the largest group to immigrate to the United States over the years has come from Germany, not England.

The emphasis in the past was on "blending" in with American culture, what began as English Enlightenment values. Immigrants committed to uphold U.S. laws. They learned English and learned to embrace the American way of life. They came here drawn to the magnet of American free enterprise as well as the other freedoms that we embrace, which they were not finding back home.

The "I-hate-the-Eurocentric-West" because of the sins of a very small minority in the past, does not represent diversity or a blending of culture; instead, it's destructive of society and divides the nation. Getting caught up in the hate and self-loathing surrounding American slavery and European colonialism ignores the fact that both slavery and colonialism have been gone for a long time. No one is alive today who lived under American slavery.

Furthermore, the "I-hate-the-Eurocentric-West" that permeates certain colleges and universities seems to forget that Hispanic culture derives from Hispania (Spain and Portugal) and is thus part of that Eurocentric West. Indeed, any "diversity" that selectively discriminates against others based on race (white), gender (male), or ethnicity (Eurocentric) doesn't represent Diversity, but rather tyranny.

Let us learn from history and condemn the evils of the past, but let us not forget the agricultural revolution that allows us today to feed 7 billion people. Let us not forget the industrial revolution that pulled billions of people out of pre-industrial poverty with life expectancy in the 40s. Let us not forget the medical revolution that has dramatically improved health worldwide and reduced infant mortality. Let us not forget the United Nations, which with all its faults has attempted to bring countries together to settle differences without resorting to war.

In addition to all of the aforementioned advances, let us not forget that every notion of progress, civil rights, individual rights, and women's rights that Americans prize is a product of the Eurocentric Enlightenment that is despised by groups within this country. Nostalgia for life before this Eurocentric culture can best be described as "nasty, brutish and short." (Thomas Hobbes)

Is that really a world to be wished for?

IMMIGRATION IMPLICATIONS

What are the implications of our immigration dilemma?

Those who wish to open U.S. borders to all in need should reflect on how the average worldwide income is around $16,400 per person. Open borders encourage economic immigration to the point that average earnings in the United States and across the world become similar. Simply put, if your income is above $16,400, you are wealthy by world standards and over time can expect your income to drop with the immigration of labor willing to work for low wages.

Foreigners know about the 14th Amendment to the Constitution. It states that "all persons born … in the United States, and subject to the jurisdiction thereof, are citizens of the United States." The prevailing interpretation is that if you are an illegal immigrant and you have a baby in the United States, that baby automatically becomes eligible for all benefits of citizenship, which includes American welfare programs. Illegal immigrants are told this before they arrive and use this law as a "loophole" to U.S. citizenship.

Not only does the child become an American citizen at birth, but we find it unconscionable and morally repugnant to separate the child from its mother. Immigrants know this as well. Thus, to gain legitimacy in the United States and enjoy all the benefits of living here, all a woman has to do is have a child in this country and she is permitted to stay and is protected from deportation. This has been an incredible magnet drawing economic immigrants.

Immigration-deniers say people aren't doing this. That attitude only denies reality in deference to unsupported mantra beliefs.

The bone of contention in the 14th Amendment is "and subject to the jurisdiction thereof." Is a child of illegal immigrants subject to the jurisdiction of the United States, given that they are here illegally? The original intent of this amendment was to make sure it applied to former slaves, not to illegal immigrants.

The United States and Canada are the only developed nations that still grant citizenship based on being born in the country. Australia and New Zealand repealed this in 2007 and 2005 respectively. Ireland was the last European country to repeal this in 2004. Outside of Latin America, almost no countries grant citizenship just based on being born within a nation's borders. Even in Latin America, Chile and Colombia do not.

Let's leave it to legal scholars to interpret the law.

The broad interpretation of the 14th Amendment has encouraged millions of people to come to the United States to have their children. It has become a license to exploit U.S. laws in order to obtain American jobs and welfare benefits, including Medicaid, at the expense of American citizens. It's the promise of a better life that brings immigrants here. It's the promise of getting the benefits that citizens have that brings illegal immigrants. Our laws and welfare programs are a magnet attracting millions of workers and their families.

The huge inflow of immigrants and in particular illegal immigrants has depressed wages for American workers (as discussed under Depressed Wages), especially in lower-paying jobs and those near minimum wage. It has also depressed wages for recent immigrants as well.

Out of compassion, you may want to help all these immigrants, but remember if you earn more than $16,400 per person ($7.89/hour), compassion calls for you to donate your excess earnings to the poor of the world. The billions of people who make less than $16,400 would love to come here and work at $8/hour.

What history shows us is that immigration in the 500,000 per year range does not appear to depress wages. Immigration at the current level of 1 million per year does.

We have reached the point in this country where there are no easy answers. There are too many groups with a vested interest in allowing high immigration and illegal immigration to continue.

- Farms need workers willing to do the seasonal harvesting that many citizens are not eager to do. Farm work is tough labor. Only 1-2% of Americans have grown up on a farm. City folk aren't attracted to seasonal backbreaking work. Some people have argued that we should pay more. That still won't attract the number of seasonal laborers needed on the farms. Besides, higher wages will lead to higher prices that will hurt the poor and the middle class.
- Companies in a variety of industries, such as those that use fiberglass, have difficulty finding Americans willing to do the work. Some businesses have looked the other way or even encouraged illegal immigrants to fill their jobs. If these companies can't find the labor, they will be forced to outsource these and all associated jobs to Mexico.
- Immigrants and families of immigrants want open immigration, preferably legal, so that they can bring more of their family members here. That's understandable, but they need to understand that more immigration will lead to lower compensation and struggles to find jobs. It is in the best interests of current immigrants to slow the pace of future immigration.
- Socially conscious individuals want open immigration since their compassion calls for them to help the poor of the world. Are you prepared to take another 10 million, another 100 million, or more? The United States will not be able to deliver on the promise of a better life if we take in too many immigrants too fast. That will lead to social unrest and to the United States no longer being the magnet it is today. In fact, if we raise the minimum wage and keep immigration high, we will be setting the stage for more disappointments and unrest, much as the Romans did with the Goths.

Despite all of the downsides of continuing with our current high levels of immigration, there are few except for the jingoists who stand up and say we should take this slower. Immigration is fine and healthy. High immigration depresses wages and makes it difficult to absorb all of the newcomers.

History shows that immigration that occurs too rapidly and for too long a period of time leads to adverse changes to the native culture. We can listen to history or become another footnote.

DEPORTATION

Some people have called for the deportation of 11 million illegal immigrants, a sizable percentage of which work in this country, many in agricultural jobs that are in need of workers.

The moral dilemma is the disruption to the lives of 11 million people. It involves potential separation of parents from their children born in this country. Deportation runs against America's sense of compassion, but compassion comes with a cost. American citizens pay the price for services for the illegal immigrants, including medical costs. In addition, Americans pay a price in lower wages since there are more workers willing to take the number of available jobs, in particular low wage jobs. On the other hand, the morality of deporting people goes well beyond the morality of not letting them in in the first place.

The legal side of this will need to be settled in the courts or by an act of Congress. Some have argued that the automatic citizenship was not intended to apply to illegal immigrants, only to America's freed slaves. The courts will have to decide, but a huge legal battle will arise with any attempt to break up families.

The economic side of this will involve the loss of workers, principally in the agricultural sector that has struggled to find laborers for planting and harvesting. It's true that these workers make less than citizens, but what they make is more than they would have back home; otherwise, they wouldn't risk coming here. In addition, there's no long line of citizens willing to work the fields at these wages, and if wages were increased to what citizens might take, that would cause food prices to skyrocket, hurting the poor and middle class.

The practical side of deportations involves rounding up millions of people, transporting them, feeding them, tending to medical issues, and housing them during the process. Where would we send them? They don't all come from Mexico. Do we send those from El Salvador back to the crisis in their country or do we dump them and the others at the border and let the Mexican government deal with them? All of the options are problematic.

The entire process of deportation sounds repugnant, reminiscent of the relocation of Native Americans in the past. Furthermore, punishing these people for the lax American immigration policies over the past 25 years is shifting the pain from those who encouraged this and looked the other way to those who only wanted to better their lives. If previous generations of Americans had done this, none of us would be here today, including the Native Americans.

IMMIGRATION OPTIONS

Immigration is perhaps one of the toughest issues America faces. Our compassion calls for us to help while reason and history tells us to slow down the pace, which is not the same as being anti-immigrant as some profess in their political mantras intended to shut off any intelligent discussion. After 25 years of the most rapid rate of immigration, we need to assimilate those who have arrived into our economy and society. If we don't, we will have failed to live up to the promises that brought them here.

How do we thread our way through this quagmire?

1. Continue to do nothing while American citizens pay for services for illegal immigrants in need and suffer from lower wages from the additional workers. This creates a two-tier society that resembles a form of slavery with an illegal underclass that is repugnant to American values.
2. Every so many years have an amnesty and pretend to fix the problem until next time. This periodically pulls the illegal underclass into the mainstream, removing the underclass until more illegal immigrants come in, encouraged by how easy it was for the last group. This was a great incentive to encourage more illegal immigrants after the amnesty of the 1980s.
3. Deport all illegal immigrants and take the economic hit and disruption as well as the moral implications. If nothing is done to stem the tide of more people coming here,

annual deportations would be necessary, dragging the moral issue out for decades.

4. Execute a comprehensive plan that shuts down illegal immigration and deals with those who are already here.

No approach to illegal immigration will be effective unless it deals with stopping more people from coming here illegally. So, what options do we have to slow down the flow of illegal immigrants?

1. Build a wall, tighten border security, and beef up the Coast Guard to stem the tide of immigrants who will then bypass the land route. Israel has shown a wall to be an effective deterrent to people illegally entering their country. It's expensive to set up and maintain, but so is having 11 million illegal immigrants in this country and the entire structure of a society based on them. On the other hand, a wall gives the appearance of siege mentality and that we are not neighborly.
2. Tighten controls on those who overstay their visas. A significant number of illegal immigrants arrive legally and stay after their visas expire.
3. Fine and penalize companies that knowingly hire illegals to get them to stop being a magnet to draw people here with jobs just so the companies can keep wages down.
4. Eliminate the inducements for illegal immigrants to come here. Create a guest-worker program for those workers needed in agriculture and remove all welfare programs to illegals who do not go through the proper immigration process. In other words, come legally (including guest-workers) and you will be eligible for programs. Come illegally and you will not. In fact, you will be deported.
5. Change the laws that grant automatic citizenship to those born in this country to illegal immigrant parents. The developed world has moved away from automatic birthright with the United States and Canada the only holdouts. Is it time to join the rest of the world on this issue and get rid of the single greatest magnet to illegal immigrants, a backdoor loophole to American citizenship?
6. Work closer with countries from which immigrants are

coming in order to help them create circumstances such that their citizens don't feel compelled to flee.

After we have a plan in place to prevent new illegal immigrants, we will still have some 11 million such individuals in this country. Many of these people have lived in this country for a long time and have obeyed all but the immigration laws. What options do we have to deal with them?

1. As discussed above, we could deport all illegal immigrants, which would break up families where the children are by birth Americans. Even if this were feasible, it's not morally or even economically the best decision for America, since that would devastate the farming industry.
2. Grant amnesty to those already here as we've done in the past in the belief that securing the border will stop future illegals. The problem with this plan is that it encourages more illegals to come here with the hope of citizenship. It also doesn't deal with the families of current illegal immigrants. There will be pressure to allow their families to immigrate, continuing the pressure on wages and assimilation. Furthermore, it doesn't deal with those among the illegals who have committed other crimes.
3. Create a path to citizenship for the illegals already here.

In order to create an effective path to citizenship, we would first screen out and deport all those individuals who have broken U.S. laws other than immigration. To discourage other illegals, we could set up reasonable penalties for breaking the immigration laws. Then those already here would need to earn citizenship in some way that is not an easy incentive that invites more to come.

Out of compassion, there are those who will say the illegal immigrants have suffered enough and should be granted citizenship without penalties, which is effectively amnesty. Their premise is that we should overlook their act of coming to this country illegally since that was in the past and these individuals have obeyed the laws since coming here. It also plays to our sense of giving people a second chance.

With that logic, are we prepared to say that a murderer should go free without penalties if he is no longer committing murder or a pedophile be released from all restrictions if he is no longer committing illegal acts? It's a slippery slope to argue for a complete pardon for illegal acts. Some form of amends would seem to make more sense as part of a comprehensive path to citizenship, and to discourage others looking for a free ride.

While we seek a path to resolve immigration, both legal and illegal, we might consider giving a higher priority to managing immigration for the benefit of the United States first and for the benefit of immigrants second.

As to which immigrants make the most sense to allow in, perhaps we could consider those with the skills to best contribute to American society and our economy, rather than on the basis of having a relative in the United States. As with other countries, the United States might decide to give preference to those with job offers in the United States and to those able to support themselves and their families over those who need welfare assistance.

Dealing with immigration will not be an easy problem to resolve, but it has been made tougher by the lack of leadership and will. So far, all actions have been to kick the problem to the next generation.

We are the next generation. We should deal with it.

PART 8: WORLD MYTHS

≈≈≈≈≈≈≈≈≈≈≈≈≈≈≈≈≈≈≈≈≈≈≈≈≈≈≈≈

NATION BUILDING IN MIDDLE EAST

Throughout history, many attempts were made to build or rebuild nations. The Founding Fathers in America were successful at birthing a new nation, though flaws in that process led to the American Civil War. Mustafa Kemal Atatürk founded the Republic of Turkey after World War I. Konrad Adenauer was successful in rebuilding Germany after World War II. All of these were insiders, and it should be noted that for the United States, the 13 colonies joined together voluntarily through a process of negotiation.

The only instance of successful regime change from the outside that comes to mind was General MacArthur in Japan after World War II. That was because he took time to understand Japanese culture and tailor his approach to their circumstances. For one, Emperor Hirohito was allowed to stay as a figurehead. The transition was made from a militaristic nation during the war into a peaceful nation afterwards. One advantage Japan had was being a homogeneous country. More on that in a minute.

By contrast, we can thank big government, big picture thinkers over the years for the mess in the Middle East. Prior to World War I, the Ottoman Empire kept the peace by allowing a fair amount of autonomy to the various communities as long as locals didn't create problems for the Ottoman Turks. After the war, France took control of what is now Syria while England took what is now Iraq. "What is now" refers to the fact that these were not countries prior to French and English control.

For the European powers, it came down to this—they didn't want to deal with the messy mosaic of Middle Eastern politics that included a wide range of ethnic groups and religions living side by side. To make life easier for themselves, they each created a centralized government to administer their protectorates. They tried to impose secular European governments over a cluster of diverse communities, disregarding local customs and competing interests.

Under the decentralized authority of Ottoman rule, Middle Eastern communities administered their own affairs with the Ottoman Turks mediating between various groups as needed. Under the central control that the European powers created for their own convenience, the diverse groups competed for power in the new central government to protect the interests of their own communities against threats from other groups, in particular against the majority populations.

In what was cobbled together as Iraq, the Sunni minority in the west was allowed by the British to gain control over the Shiite majority in the southeast and the Kurds in the north, imposing their rule under an autocratic regime. That continued until the United States stepped in to topple Hussein with no plan as to what to do next. Using Western democratic traditions, this regime change allowed the Shiite majority to take control.

From the standpoint of promoting democracy, that seemed to make sense. However, after the Shiites gained power, they sought to make up for decades of subjugation under Sunni rule by diminishing the role of the minority group. Stripped of power, many Sunnis turned to terrorist groups to protect their interests in a Shiite-dominated country. It's hard to go from top dog to underdog in your own country.

The Syrian story is similar with France ignoring the delicate balance of diverse communities in their attempt to impose a European-style secular government on a fractured and very religious region. The minority coastal Alawites in the northwest, along with allies concerned about a new government being controlled by the Sunni majority, managed to take control and impose their autocratic rule over the majority. Assad and his father resorted to violence against their citizens in order to hold onto power.

The Arab Spring gave the Syrian Sunnis a glimpse of being able to overthrow Assad in order to protect their interests. Assad's allies in Iran and Russia came to his support. Now the Sunnis in Syria risk defeat and retributions from the minority controlled government of Assad. Many have turned to terrorist and other militant groups for help.

The problem with the secular democracies imposed on this region is the nuanced ethnic and religious interrelationships developed over a long history between these groups.

The solution is simple and not so simple.

We could help Syria and Iraq to return to decentralized authority as they had under the Ottoman Empire. Without an outside power like Turkey to oversee conflict between the many groups, there will continue to be a struggle to control whatever government emerges over these two cobbled-together countries.

An alternative would be to divide Syria and Iraq along major ethnic lines. Let the Shiites have a country in the southeast of what is Iraq. The Kurds could have their own nation in the north, while the Sunnis would govern in the west. A similar split could be made for Syria, with the Alawites and their allies having their own country in the northwest and west, the Kurds being allowed to join the Kurds from Iraq, and the Sunnis controlling the rest of what is Syria, perhaps in union with the Iraqi Sunnis.

Aside from the inertia from those who already hold power, there are several problems with splitting up these countries. The big one is that Turkey would resist the creation of a Kurdish state on its border. A large portion of eastern Turkey contains Kurdish people struggling for autonomy or independence from the Turkish government. A second issue is that replacing two countries with four or more would not end the sectarian fighting between these groups. A third issue is that of minorities caught in the middle of any division and in particular Baghdad and Damascus, which contain many ethnic groups.

The biggest problem is that this solution does not appear feasible from the inside. Those who control the levers of power over each of the current countries will not readily agree to anything less. Countries rarely split apart peacefully. Even India's split into India and Pakistan was painful.

To be successful, change would have to be guided or imposed from the outside. Given the nature and duration of the conflicts, it would be difficult to find any outside power who could gain the trust of all the parties to get to a solution. Perhaps this option could have been put into place at the time of the fall of Hussein, but that opportunity has passed.

At that time, in deference to Turkish interests with regard to their Kurds, it was not considered. In addition, there was distrust of the Iraqi Sunnis who had been in power under Hussein.

A broader solution that carved Kurdistan out of portions of Iraq, Syria, Turkey, and Iran would weaken Turkey, a key Western ally. Making any split even more difficult would be the allocation of resources. Most of the oil resources of Iraq are in the southeast (Shiite area) and in the north (Kurdish area that the Sunnis would fight for). Splitting Syria along ethnic lines would give the Alawites and their allies the port cities and Damascus, leaving the Sunnis landlocked with few resources.

Any solution that ignores the needs of the Sunnis is doomed to failure and they are out of power in both Iraq and Syria. Giving them autonomy or their own country is the only solution that addresses their interests.

In summary, the region will continue to be in conflict until a new political arrangement emerges that considers the diverse interests or suppresses them. Let us hope it's not the latter.

REGIME CHANGE

What makes for successful regime change?

We make the mistake in the United States of looking at myths surrounding the American Revolution that happened so many years ago, and trying to apply that to other countries. There is no international comparison to the American Revolution. What made this revolution different than all the others was:

1. Meaning no disrespect to the Native Americans, as regards the relevant factors of the American Revolution, the United States was established on new land. It was not created as a replacement of a regime in an existing country, which describes most other examples of nation building. In other words, it was nation building and not regime change. In this regard, it was not unlike wars of independence throughout the rest of the Americas, though very different than changes elsewhere. Although the Native Americans were disadvantaged by the new settlers, relative to the revolution, there was no long heritage of an entitled ruling class that was overthrown as part of the Revolution.
2. The colonies grew up under British common law and took inspiration from the Enlightenment. Both guided not only the institutions the Founding Fathers created afterwards, but also the broad participation of people in the revolution itself. This was not a rebellion by a handful of terrorists or a privileged few.

3. The power from which Americans were declaring independence was thousands of miles away. This is an important point when comparing this to the French or Russian revolutions. The colonies were not rebelling against a central government on this continent but rather overseas. In that sense, it has some similarity to other wars of independence from colonial rule.

When we look at countries in the Middle East or Libya, we are seeing lands with thousand-year traditions. These lands have a local entitled class that has ruled over others who bear long grievances for vengeance if they ever achieve power themselves. Instead of an uprising of the people, these rebellions are often driven by strongmen jockeying for power.

In a unique act of statesmanship, the first leader of the new American republic, George Washington, stepped down after 8 years as President in deference to building democratic institutions. Yet, in so many other rebellions and regime changes, leaders have clung to power for decades or been deposed when they refused to step down. In the Middle East, long-held grievances from the past make it difficult for rebel groups to come together to form a government and thus, new strongmen take over, replacing the strongmen they deposed.

Unless we find players who really understand the dynamics of the local situation and are prepared to develop a process that addresses the diverse and competing interests in the Middle East, it will be nearly impossible to help those countries to move beyond addressing grievances of the past in order to move forward. As a consequence, we should tread very carefully before we venture into another regime change opportunity. The unintended consequences, as in Iraq and Libya, could leave us worse off than before.

We should be certain we have a plan before we proceed with any action against Assad.

WAR

Since we are a nation whose people long for peace, why not take war off the table?

In the 1970s there was a slogan along the lines of: What if they gave a war and we didn't show up. Well, let's see. What if we were in a basketball championship and didn't show up? What if we were in the Super Bowl and failed to show. Yep, we'd forfeit, a nice way of saying, "You lose."

Peace itself cannot be your sole objective or you will surrender to terror. Neville Chamberlain, in the vain pursuit of peace with Germany, delayed action until a catastrophe was inevitable and far costlier.

Peaceniks say we have a strong military we should commit never to use. Of course, if we'll never use it, why not save the cost and just pretend we have a military since wishing for peace should be enough. Why get our hands dirty?

On the other hand, we have the overeager cowboys. No matter how clear it is to the rest of us that military action isn't the right solution for a particular situation, they swing into action to show they have brass. Boy did we show Hussein. The trouble is that the mess we have today is worse than what we had before and look at what it cost us.

Before the Soviet Afghan War, the Soviet Union appeared to be a major international threat. They failed in Afghanistan. For decades afterwards, they fell into decline. Let us hope that is not the price America is facing for the hubris of replacing Hussein without a viable plan.

Teddy Roosevelt said to "Speak softly and carry a big stick." He didn't get America into foreign wars, but in 1904 when Barbary Pirates operating in Morocco kidnapped a Greek-American citizen, Roosevelt sent in a navy squadron to pressure the Moroccan government to resolve the issue. The issue was resolved without American bloodshed.

A good leader knows that we shouldn't hop into every conflict to show off our military strength. After all, why wear ourselves out on skirmishes if we don't have to. The clever leader even knows how to grab victory from the jaws of defeat.

As an example, look at Russia from 1550 to 1721. They were in almost a constant state of warfare on several fronts. They faced multiple defeats and yet through negotiation and stubbornness, they emerged stronger and larger.

The point being that we give up too much if we take war off the table. Yet, we risk too much in war, both as to cost and uncertainty, such that it should be used as a last resort, and at times as leverage in negotiations.

We should only go to war when we are prepared to commit to goals. If war is necessary, we should minimize civilian casualties, yet accept that when our enemies hide behind civilians, civilians will die.

War should be the last option, but never taken off the table.

TERRORISM BACKGROUND

Under Nation Building and Regime Change we talked about how we got into the mess in the Middle East. What does that mean for the terror threat?

Most people in all societies want to be left alone to lead their lives without interference from neighbors, overlords, or outsiders. Left alone, they'll live in peace until something stirs them up with threats to their livelihoods and beliefs.

Yet, in any group, we can count on some one percent who will find themselves discontented. That applies to every religious group, every ethnic group, and every social group. Circumstances are not to their liking. They are unhappy and rather than seeking to improve their lives by working harder and smarter and living in peace, they are either motivated and agitated enough to stir things up themselves or susceptible to being riled up by others.

Perhaps they feel like social outcasts even in their own group. Maybe they have skills that they don't feel are recognized or appreciated, such as charisma or social manipulation skills. Using those skills to upset the world around them gives them a sense of value and purpose.

In any case, we find these people in every society. It's therefore not surprising we find a small group of Muslim extremists who have joined terror groups. They enjoy the power to manipulate and to prove to themselves and to the world that they matter.

Whether these individuals rise to great power as Hitler did will depend on circumstances. The previously discussed policies in

Syria and Iraq have provided the perfect environment for today's terrorists. Whether they will succeed in disrupting the entire world depends on how well they are understood and dealt with. The "bomb-them-back-to-the-stone-age" approach won't work. They would relish a playing field they believe gives them an advantage.

Perhaps some historical perspective would help.

Vikings were the terrorists of their day, raiding towns and monasteries. They sailed into France and took over Normandy. Then they conquered England and ruled for hundreds of years. Their presence led to the Hundred-Years War as their descendants fought to hold onto French lands.

In the east, the Viking "Rus" from what is now Sweden took over Russia and helped to create Russian kingdoms, with them at the top. Viking terror didn't end until they converted to Christianity and stopped raiding the Christian nations of Europe.

Why is this important today? Viking terror wasn't defeated until they became part of the broader European society.

More recently, Mahatma Gandhi took a decidedly non-terrorist approach. He took on the powerful British Empire and won Indian independence by using non-violent civil disobedience. Would that have succeeded against Nazi Germany? Would it have done as well against Japan during World War II? Not a chance. Neither regime had any qualms about killing millions of civilians. Britain did. Gandhi studied in England. He learned about civil disobedience and British culture. He then used his enemy's weaknesses against them and won.

Why does this matter?

Many within the terrorist groups have studied the West. They have learned about our culture and our weaknesses. They are using those weaknesses against us, including our own technology and social media. They are also using against us our aversion to civilian casualties, when they use human shields. They use against us our "leave-no-one-behind" policy, which has given them leverage by kidnapping people.

When they want a prisoner released, they kidnap someone for a trade. They have been effective in using our policies to inflict casualties and in negotiations to gain the release of several dangerous combatants in exchange for a single American soldier or civilian. Notice how every prisoner exchange includes many of their combatants for every single American. America's enemies know how to play this game.

Most people come to this country for opportunity. Many come with high expectations, some with unrealistic expectations. If only one percent of any population is dissatisfied, particularly when faced with stagnant wages, how many will rise up in anger over dashed expectations, feeling that they are discriminated against because their expectations were too high?

America needs to act prudently and yet we should take a lesson from the British during World War II. They adopted a "Keep calm and carry on" approach to air-raid sirens and daily bombardment from the Germans, staying alert and yet continuing with their lives. They did not let terror turn them into nervous mice.

Some of those who call for calm, say the answer is for the American people to keep watch and report anything suspicious. What's interesting is that many of those who slap Islamophobia on anyone who even hints at restricting immigration are the same people who slap the same label on anyone who reports suspicious activity, as happened with a boy who brought a suspicious clock to school.

Who, except an expert, would be in a position to determine if that was innocent experimentation or a test of America's response? What is certain is that the backlash against reporting suspicious activities plays into the hands of the terrorists who probe for weaknesses in America's security.

TERRORISM ISSUES

What issues do we face in dealing with terrorism today?

A big hole in American security has surfaced in the encrypted emails and online communications. This is a no-win situation. Either these communications are encrypted or they aren't.

The selling point to legitimate people using encryption is that no one other than intended parties can read the encrypted messages. This is important for banking and payment transactions and protection of passwords. If there's a backdoor that allows the government to peek, then encryption fails its objective. People wanting privacy will search for encryption that can't be hacked, and there are plenty of people out there willing to create that software. In addition, if there's a backdoor the government can use, hackers will find it and sell it on the dark Internet.

If the encryption holds, to protect privacy, then there's no way for the software companies to open these for the government. In this case, terrorists will be using our fabulous technologies, our customs, and our values against us in the same way that Gandhi won against Britain. Even with the best possible laws and practices, it will be very difficult to bridge the divide. Either encryption does its job and we lose security or it doesn't and we lose privacy.

You'd better believe the terrorists know this. Many of them trained in the West.

While Americans value their civil liberties and privacy, they also value security. Part of the challenge is accepting the fact that we are in a state of war with the terrorists. They have declared war on America and the West; they hold land and have resources. If America loses this war, there will be no more American values. There will be no more women's rights or the liberties we take for granted. There will be no more diversity rights as we understand it.

Although only a few extremist Muslims are behind this terrorist threat, America will have to thread a very tight needle to work its way through this crisis without doing what the terrorists want most, which is to goad America into turning this into a war between all Muslims and the West. That will serve the terrorists, not the peoples of the Middle East or the West.

To win this struggle, America will need to recognize those aspects of its culture and values that the terrorists are exploiting and figure out how to counter their actions. America does not need a demagogue. Neither does it need a Neville Chamberlain focused on peace at any cost.

MIDDLE EAST

Perhaps the greatest of Western hubris after World War I was the imposition by the French and British in the Middle East of centralized, secular, westernized governments.

The Middle East has had a long tradition of strong and conflicting religious beliefs that for centuries adapted to a fragile state of co-existence. These religious traditions have included not only Christians, Muslims, and Jews, but subgroups within those broad categories that today include Shiites and Sunnis, both Muslims, though with conflicting traditions.

That fragile co-existence shattered with the collapse of the Ottoman Empire and the European oversight of the area. The biggest errors, as discussed earlier, were the cobbled-together states of Syria and Iraq in the model of European traditions.

The problem with bringing Western institutions was that the Middle East never went through the European Enlightenment. It never went through the European struggles with secular democracy. These are great traditions, but perhaps we are paying the price today for the placement of secular, centralized governments based on the European model across the region from Iran to Egypt.

At the time, leaders did this with the thought of providing the gifts of European progress and its evolution of political systems. The Middle Eastern nations are now struggling with the same clash of values that Europe underwent in the eighteenth century between secular progress and religious tradition. On top of that, they are dealing with these issues in countries drawn not by their traditions, but by the nation-building of colonial powers.

It's too late to turn back the clock and start over, but we should be aware of how messy the European struggles were, including the Thirty Years War in the 17th Century that attempted to settle religious differences between the Catholics and Protestants. That struggle is not unlike what the Sunnis and Shiites are dealing with today.

The Middle East is a complex mosaic that is like the shifting sands, never the same and yet still made of the same stuff. We cannot treat conflicts in this region as we have anywhere else, and certainly not without understanding their complicated context.

RUSSIA

Americans have a very shallow understanding of Russia, based, if at all, on the cold war. Since Russians are Europeans, on the periphery of the culture that created the United States, we imagine that we know them.

Do we?

Over 1,000 years ago, the Slavic lands of what is now Russia were small farming communities. To ensure peace between them and their warring neighbors, local Slavic tribes invited the "Rus" (Viking tribes from Sweden) to rule over them. As the Rus migrated into the region, they created great walled cities like Kiev to support their river and overland trade with the Byzantine Empire to the south. For the most part, the Viking Rus focused on their cities and trade, leaving the local Slavs to their farms.

Around 988, the Kievan Tsar Vladimir (Swedish Valdemar) converted to Orthodox Christianity and proceeded with autocratic rule that married church and state. That continued until the Mongols invaded in the 13th century. The Mongols ruled for over 200 years before the Russian duchy of Muscovy gained independence. Between then and World War I, Muscovy grew to become the Russian Empire, stretching from the border of Poland to the Pacific Ocean.

At no time during this history were there any of the democratizing influences that the rest of Europe experienced. The Russian people went from being ruled by the Viking Rus, to rule under a tsar, rule by the Mongols, and more rule under the tsar. In

1917, during the Russian Revolution, they overthrew the tsar, but Russia lacked the experience or infrastructure for rule other than through autocratic means. It was, therefore, easy for Lenin and then Stalin with their disciplined communists to sweep away the budding democratic majority and replace it with another autocratic regime.

Many in the West cheered when the Soviet Union collapsed in the 1980s and Russia appeared headed toward Western European democratic enlightenment. As we've seen, that has not happened.

Russia is not Western Europe or the United States. It has not experienced the Enlightenment and the other struggles that molded us into the people we are today. That's not to say they can't learn from our experiences, but Russian experience carries more resignation to the harsh realities of Russian winters, threats from neighbors, tough Russian leaders, and nationalism.

As a modern state, Russia begins perhaps with the Duchy of Muscovy (modern day Moscow), not long before the settlement of what would become the United States. The paths both nations took were radically different. While the United States grew westward under democratic institutions, Russia grew toward the east, including Alaska under the rule of the tsar.

Prior to the Civil War, the United States grew based on individual ownership of property, and in the South with agriculture based on slaves. During this time, Russia struggled to copy European industrialization, but mostly maintained its farm-based community with feudal lords and serfs (like slaves) tied to the land and the landowner. In fact, the Russians freed their serfs about the same time as Americans freed their slaves. That's about the extent of the similarities.

A mere 50 some years after the American Civil War, the Soviet government in Russia took away private ownership, returning farmers to their earlier serf-like status of working for government managed farms. Farmers who resisted were killed by the thousands. In the cities, workers became part of collective ownership of production that was controlled by an autocratic leader under a new title.

Over the years, fear of outsiders has been a constant concern for Russians, from the treatment at the hands of neighbors in the early years, to the Mongol invasion, and then to Napoleon in 1812. That fear was capped off by terrible losses in World War I, foreign invaders after the war who tried to stop the communist takeover, and then even worse losses in World War II. The fear of being besieged has created a nationalistic fervor for a people who have lacked the freedoms we in the West take for granted.

Taken in this light, the Russians fear a strong Germany. They worry about a strong European Community to their west and the eastward encroachment of NATO to include Poland, Hungary, and other countries that previously were under Russian control. They took very personally the attempt by Ukraine to join the European Block. That was the motivation for Russia to grab the Crimea and to intervene in eastern Ukraine. And the Russian people support this out of their fear of outsiders and encirclement.

There's a lot of bravado from some candidates about standing up to Russia, but pay heed to Russian history and traditions. If you stand up to a grizzly bear with your bare hands, that won't go well. Russia is a bear.

They feel encircled, a remnant from the West's containment policies of the past century. These traits are what motivated Russia to intervene in the Middle East, which borders Russia to the south and which they consider part of their neighborhood. To them, this is a defensive move to protect their interests.

That doesn't mean that America should stand by and let Russia have their way, but we need to recognize who we are dealing with in order to be effective. They do not share American traditions or values. Yet, if we can find common cause with Russia and address their security concerns that could go a long way toward working together to deal with the Middle East problems. If we continue the cold war policy of containment, we will encourage their nationalistic fight to protect Russia's neighborhood.

CHINA

China remains a mystery to us as well it would. Chinese culture dates back more than 2,000 years to the Han Dynasty. It had ups and downs over the centuries but the Chinese have retained their own distinct culture. So what should we know about the Chinese in order to deal with the growing conflicts in Asia?

The Chinese refer to themselves as the "Middle Kingdom" and throughout most of history they have been the center of the universe they cared about. A little known fact is that Chinese explorers sailed to the Americas before Columbus. They very well might have pressed their claim except the presiding emperor died and the new emperor focused energies on China rather than exploration. He chose isolationism.

Turning inward meant that during the 19th Century, China suffered humiliations at the hands of colonial powers. Then they were invaded by Japan prior to and during World War II.

In 1949, the communists took over in China, bringing an ideology imported from Russia. At first, they used it along Russian lines but over time it took on a Chinese flavor uniquely adapted to their culture. As they have moved to a more entrepreneurial economy, many in the United States cheered that they were joining the capitalist fold. Don't hold your breath.

What we are witnessing is a blending of traditional Chinese culture, socialist aspects of their communist days, and an entrepreneurial spirit that predates the United States. In other words, China is importing ideas and combining them into what will become a new Chinese culture that will not resemble America. We need to understand and respect this.

Over the centuries, China has united as it did during the Han Dynasty 2,000 years ago, and fractured into little fiefdoms, speaking diverse dialects of Chinese that are not universally understood. Yet, even during its decentralized days, they have retained a uniquely Chinese identity that is unlike the fractured identities of Europe or those of the Indian subcontinent. In part, this might be due to 90% of Chinese being Han Chinese, which provides a strong ethnic unity.

Over the years China was invaded by the Mongols and later by the colonial powers. While Britain left her mark on India in terms of language and institutions, China retained its own institutions and culture even in the face of invasions. That is how strong the Chinese core is.

During thousands of years as the Middle Kingdom, China expected tribute and deference from surrounding nations like Korea, Vietnam, and Formosa (now Taiwan). The Middle Kingdom owned the South China Sea and only lost it when European colonialists came and then Japan's power rose.

Looked at in this light, China's recent actions in the South China Sea represent to them merely recovering what was lost. Failing to understand this as we search for a solution to the conflict in the area will risk miscalculations that could lead to a war neither country wants.

An interesting aspect of China's colonial experience was that the United States did not participate in exploiting China since the United States was focused on internal development. America was not part of the colonial humiliations China suffered. During World War II, the United States helped China to push back Japanese aggression and defeat China's enemy. This won the United States much goodwill in China. That goodwill was eroded by U.S. opposition to the communists taking over in China and then siding with Nationalist China on Taiwan, a land that China sees as part of Greater China.

We should consider some parallels from history.

At the beginning of the 20th Century, Germany was an emerging economic power. Britain, France, and others with their colonial empires and mercantile trading systems tried to block Germany as a growing threat. Not giving Germany a seat at the table as much as anything led to World War I. Mid-century, Germany asserted herself again with disastrous results. Today, the German economy dominates Europe. It can be argued that both world wars were about adapting to Germany's economic role in Europe and Japan's role in Asia.

It would be a mistake to believe that we could exclude China from asserting her role as a global power with the second largest economy in the world and the world's largest population. Let us not repeat the mistakes of the 20th Century with Germany.

It would behoove the United States to find common ground with China and understand the world from its perspective before we proceed in trying to impose our view. That's not to say that China should be allowed to take what they want, but as with any good negotiation, we need to understand what's important to the other side.

CHINA & CYBERWARFARE

Cyberwarfare has become the 21st Century counterpart to the tank, the airplane, the machine gun, and other innovations that upset the balance of power in the world.

In the past, new military technologies have led to warfare as nations adjusted to the new realities and what they meant to their positions in the world. Germany would not have been the threat they were during World War II without blitzkrieg warfare that depended on their air force and their mobile tank divisions.

Now cyberwarfare has become another aggressive tool of military diplomacy, not unlike the atomic bomb. Both weapons can cause significant damage and destroy lives, though cyberwarfare's role is more subtle and behind the scenes.

For those who don't believe the seriousness of the threat from cyberwarfare, imagine waking up tomorrow and the electric grid is gone. With no electricity to run the pumps, the water supply fails. While the effects of cyber threats could be more far reaching, just this one aspect should illustrate the seriousness of the threat. How long can Americans living in cities go with no water?

Cyberwarfare has turned into a cops-and-robbers game. No matter what security we develop, the hackers will find a way around it. Tackling this issue will require the recognition that it's an important threat. It will also require coordination between technology companies and governments working through laws to find ways to protect American institutions and infrastructure, while also protecting the privacy rights of our citizens.

Chinese, working with and without their government's knowledge and help, are breaking into the security systems of American companies to steal trade secrets and proprietary information so that they can steal American research and development to further their goals. They use this information to help them buy up American companies, using money they've gained through the vast trade imbalance to buy America with its own money.

There's bravado from some candidates about how we need to stand up to China in the South China Sea, but can we even depend on the electronics that all of our systems hinge on in time of crisis? Our dependence on technology in general and components received from China threatens to undermine any posturing America might make and could lead to miscalculations and an unnecessary war.

Somehow, America needs to remain at the forefront of technology and electronic security if we hope to remain a strong, secure nation with a vibrant economy that creates jobs.

PART 9: ABRUPT CLIMATE CHANGE

≈≈

CLIMATE CHANGE HISTORY

Climate change and climate science is a fabrication of big-government types who have a solution (more government control) and are using climate change to justify policies they support. So say climate-deniers.

Unfortunately for the deniers, there's a long history of abrupt climate change. If humans do send climate out of control, they won't be the first. Eons ago, anaerobic bacteria thrived on Earth. Those are bacteria that don't breathe oxygen, though they do produce oxygen as a byproduct. They were so successful that they increased the concentration of oxygen in Earth's atmosphere to the point that it was toxic to them and now they only thrive in oxygen-free environments underground and in our guts.

Perhaps we should pay attention.

Around 10,000 years ago, glaciers that covered much of Europe and North America melted. That allowed for forests and the settlement of humans across Europe. In the absence of that, we would not be looking at the United States that we know today.

While Europe and North America lay beneath a mile of ice, the Sahara still bloomed, supporting human communities. Then around 5,500 years ago, there was a shift in the Earth's tilt. That might have been a result of the melting glaciers, which moved the mass of frozen water from the north to the warmer oceans farther south. In any case, the Sahara region dried out and those gardens turned into the Sahara Desert that covers about a third of the African continent.

In America around 1130-1180, the Pueblo Indians at Chaco Canyon and Mesa Verde in the Southwest faced a prolonged drought. That forced them to abandon the area, leaving behind the canals that formed the basis of Phoenix's initial water system.

There was a Medieval Warm Period in Europe from 900 to 1300 AD that enriched agriculture in the far north. This enabled the Vikings to become prosperous and spread out across Europe, Russia, and the North Atlantic. They were even able to raise livestock in the grasslands of Greenland. Around 1200 AD, temperatures dropped to where they had to abandon their Greenland settlements. Colder temperatures coincided with a general decline in Viking influence.

Around 1200 AD, there was a warming period with more rainfall in the steppes of Asia. That coincided with the rise of the Mongol culture and allowed them to expand from a prosperous core to conquer the largest contiguous land empire in the world.

The Little Ice Age began suddenly in the 1300s. Temperatures in the northern hemisphere dropped 1-2 degrees centigrade. It doesn't seem like much, but the general cooling led to famines across Europe and plagues. It wasn't until the mid-1800s that the temperatures began to rise, this time aided by side-effects of the industrial revolution.

There are those who point to the rise in temperatures from the low point 200 years ago as justification for their belief in man-made climate change. Others point to the longer view as described above and say it just isn't so. Yet there is ample evidence that abrupt climate change has taken place over the long history of the Earth.

Today's worldwide temperatures are already approaching the peaks of the last interglaciation period about 130,000 years ago, and the one before that about 400,000 years ago. For the first time in a very long time, the Northwest Passage was open in 2007 and 2010. At the same time, carbon dioxide levels in the atmosphere continue to climb to levels not seen in the past 400,000 years. During the last two interglaciation peaks, sea levels were 13-20 feet above today's levels. That would be catastrophic to many coastal cities.

Prior abrupt climate change has been associated with changes in the tilt of Earth's orbit, significant volcanic activity, changes in the sun's brightness, and sunspots. Whatever else the Earth and

Sun might throw at us, this time will have the added push of human activity.

Whether one believes humans created the current warming or not, we need only look at history and pre-history to understand the effects of abrupt climate change. Those brought glaciers that covered Europe and North America prior to 10,000 years ago. Abrupt climate change also turned the lush gardens of North Africa into the Sahara Desert. If either were to happen to the United States, this country would no longer be the great nation it is today.

To those who will say this won't happen in their lifetimes, I would point out that the Little Ice Age swept in over a period of a decade.

HUMANS & CLIMATE CHANGE

There are those who say, "Okay, maybe climate is changing, but humans have no impact on it." Evidently, these people believe that no matter what we do, climate is too big and mere humans can have no effect on their environment.

Really?

How many of us live in a house, condo, apartment, or other structure that occurs naturally, meaning not manufactured by human effort, and do so with no heating or air-conditioning?

Clusters of homes and other human developments create urban heat sinks that are hotter than the surrounding areas. If you don't believe this, visit any major city in the summertime and look at temperatures in the city and in the surrounding countryside. The same variation occurs in the winter. Cities increase temperatures. That's not a theory. It is not an opinion. It's observable fact.

So is the increase of carbon dioxide in the atmosphere. Carbon dioxide is a greenhouse gas, which has been demonstrated in the lab. Humans put billions of tons of carbon dioxide into the atmosphere by burning coal, oil, and gasoline. There are those who would say that "the solution to pollution is dilution."

On a small scale, this may be true, but humans have been producing increasing quantities of carbon dioxide, just as anaerobic bacteria eons ago became successful putting out oxygen until it became toxic to them. Isn't it possible that we're producing carbon dioxide faster than the Earth can absorb it? The levels in the atmosphere support this conclusion.

Two hundred years ago, before we began consuming oil and coal at such high levels, those billions of tons of carbon dioxide were locked up underground. Now they're in the atmosphere, and we continue to pull up more oil and coal each year. There are those who would claim that the oceans can absorb the carbon dioxide, but that increases the acidity of the oceans, which over time is reducing the amount of seafood available for human consumption. Either way, there is a cost (side-effect) associated with continuing to put out high levels of carbon dioxide from our current carbon-based economy.

Do we really want to put the future of America and the world at risk based on the belief that human activities cannot overwhelm the atmosphere and the oceans?

As with all sciences, climate science has evolved and continues to do so, responding and adapting to new data. Over the years, that adaptation to new information may have created confusion among those who choose not to believe, but climate science is at least exploring, challenging the data, and fine-tuning its analysis.

Those who deny climate science offer a long list of challenges. They claim that climate science is riddled with errors. They point to a minority opinion some 50 years ago that claimed we were heading toward another ice age. Climate science proved that claim to be flawed. Yet, deniers keep bringing this up as if it represents a flaw in today's climate science.

Deniers have pointed to sunspot cycles going back to Galileo as proving that sunspots caused the Little Ice Age, and that we can expect another cooling to begin around 2020. The Little Ice Age occurred centuries before Galileo's data.

Each time that deniers have pointed out errors, the scientific community has examined the evidence. They have corrected any errors and pointed out any flaws in denier challenges. Still, after errors are corrected or proven false, climate-deniers move on to other challenges on the theory that eventually they will find a way to unravel the science.

The challenges are welcome in their ability to make the science stronger, but the deniers seem to be motivated from a conclusion (let's not worry about climate because I love my oil) and not from the data. Let's work together to make climate science more accurate instead of denying that science has any ability to understand climate because individuals in the past have made mistakes.

Then let's move beyond denying climate science and toward what makes economic sense to make this country stronger regardless of whether climate science is right or wrong.

If you still can't wrap your head around abrupt climate change, consider an insurance policy in case climate science is correct. After all, we buy life insurance, health insurance, homeowners insurance, and car insurance to hedge against catastrophic events. Why not an insurance policy against climate science being right?

What would it cost you to accept climate science on face value? If climate science turns out to be wrong, you'll be vindicated in your beliefs. If it turns out to be correct as most scientists believe, then actions taken today could prevent the United States from facing a glacial or desert future that would destroy this great nation.

Defer the question of what actions might be worth taking and simply answer what it would cost you to work with climate science.

CLIMATE CHANGE OPTIONS

If we can agree that climate science has something to tell us about the world we live in, then perhaps we can look at the question of what humans can do about it without destroying our economy and killing jobs.

1. We could choose to do nothing and let nature take its course, though doing nothing runs counter to human nature. As a species, we build homes, dams, and invent air conditioning because we are motivated to change our environment to suit our needs. Why not with climate change as well? The upside of doing nothing is that it costs nothing except more flooding and droughts, and the loss of seafood. The downside of doing nothing is that climate will change due to both natural cycles and human activity. If we do nothing now, then when the climate does change enough, humans will do what they always do: scramble to survive. With the world's population at 7 billion, going to 10 billion, climate stress will bring famines, worldwide conflict, and wars of desperation the likes of which humans have never seen before. That is the real downside of doing nothing. America will not be able to insulate herself from that catastrophe.
2. We could place a heavy carbon tax on coal and oil. That tax would be passed on to consumers (mostly poor and middle class) with the intent of getting people to use less. After all, if it doesn't incentivize us to use less, there's no

point in the tax. The knee-jerk political reaction to higher costs on the poor and middle class will be to subsidize them so they feel no pain. With no pain, they will have limited incentive to reduce their use of products that consume coal and oil, which would defeat the purpose of the tax. In fact, any tax that is not revenue neutral will reduce economic activity as people tightened their belts to deal with higher prices resulting from the new tax. That would reduce jobs, which would hurt the poor and middle class. Ah, maybe you believe corporations will pay. Look at comments under Big Legal Awards about what "making corporations pay" really means. In the end, when corporations get charged, people pay, including customers, employees, and retirement funds as well as owners. Another side-effect of a carbon tax would be to penalize energy intensive companies like food processors and aluminum production, making them less competitive and thus costing jobs.

3. We could promote more use of corn-ethanol, which is a great boon for corn farmers. Sugar-ethanol would be better, but sugarcane doesn't grow in corn fields. The problem is that carbon emitted in growing the corn and processing it reduces the carbon benefit of using ethanol, and corn is not as efficient as sugarcane for ethanol production. We could buy from the Brazilians, but that would leave us dependent on imports again.
4. We could encourage the development and use of alternative energy sources like wind and solar. The great weakness of these sources is that they depend on the availability of sunshine and wind. At night when there's no sunlight and winds die down, there is no energy source. One solution would be to encourage an Apollo-type commitment to develop more energy efficient wind and solar collectors, and more effective storage technologies. The United States could take an economic leadership role in this instead of following countries like China and Denmark. A side benefit of developing a more effective solar/wind capability is to reduce our dependence on oil from troubled parts of the world and help our allies to do the same. Done properly, this could be a job-creating,

economy-stimulating force for the U.S. economy, returning America to the forefront of energy technology development. As a side-note, using solar for air conditioning would be a perfect fit since the greatest need for air conditioning is during sunny days.

5. We could develop a safer version of nuclear power, perhaps the thorium-based power plant. It would produce no carbon dioxide, which should make the climate change people happy, yet doesn't. This new type of plant holds several advantages over existing nuclear plants. Thorium is more plentiful than uranium. This type of plant would produce less nuclear waste and have superior properties to current reactors, including safety. Unfortunately, there are significant start-up costs and significant opposition from anti-nuclear, climate change supporters.

Each of these approaches to climate change have apparent advantages, but they all fail to address the number one cause of carbon dioxide and other greenhouse gases in the atmosphere.

REAL CAUSE OF CLIMATE CHANGE

What is the root cause of human produced climate change?

Let's say that every human today produced an average of 100 units of carbon footprint and that we were able to reduce that by 30% to 70 units by the middle of the century. Let's assume that we do that even while billions of people enjoy rising standards of living. To offset the impact of higher living standards will require an even greater reduction in carbon usage. To do this would require a tremendous effort and we might consider that a great accomplishment.

At the same time that we are performing the Herculean effort of reducing the average human footprint and raising standards of living, we are also growing the human population from 7 billion to 10 billion.

Let's look at the simple, yet inconvenient math. A hundred units of carbon times 7 billion people (700 billion units) is the same amount as 70 units times 10 billion people (700 billion units). In other words, despite all the efforts and expenditures and disruption of economies to get a 30% reduction in carbon use per person even while raising the standards of living, we would not have reduced the overall carbon emissions at all. Of course, if we did nothing, the situation would be much worse.

It's politically incorrect to say, but "The root cause of human impact on climate change and the environment is human population." This can be seen in the clearing of jungles in Brazil, Africa, and Indonesia, and in humans pushing into wilderness habitats all over the world. It can be seen in the United States with cities sprawling farther and farther into the countryside.

Not only do humans cause environmental change, but growing populations create increasing change.

Yet, with the exception of the Chinese and the naturally declining populations in the developed world, no one wants to address the population problem. Even the Chinese have reversed their one-child policy. Interestingly, those who fight hardest against accepting climate change are often the same people who are having the large families that are putting pressure on the environment. Perhaps they understand the connection.

Thus, we can come up with the most ambitious of grandiose schemes to reduce the per capita carbon footprint. If we can't address the population, it won't matter.

Even so, promoting cleaner nuclear, solar, wind, and storage technologies would make the United States an energy leader in the 21st Century. While we do this, we should tread carefully not to burden the economy with heavy new taxes that will trickle down to fewer jobs. Destroying the U.S. economy on the altar of green energy makes no sense and will weaken the nation's ability to deal with climate crises in the future.

Instead, why not encourage and provide incentives to Americans and the private sector to look at alternative energy, including new and safer nuclear energy, instead of punishing them for our past dependence on carbon. Remember that anything that abruptly blocks the oil and coal industries in this country will ripple through the economy and cost jobs.

ENERGY

While energy has implications for climate change, it also has other economic consequences, particularly related to dependence on imported oil. So, why has America been slow to adopt new energy options?

The oil embargo of 1973 should have been more of a wakeup call to America and its dependence on oil from an unstable region. Instead, the United States continued to import oil and paid exorbitant prices for energy that resulted in heavy trade losses and trillions of dollars being siphoned out of America and into the Middle East.

Over the past 42 years, Denmark, a nation of 5 million people, made great strides to eliminate their dependence on Middle Eastern oil. Yet, it wasn't until very recently that the United States, through offshore drilling, fracking, and finally alternative energy sources, began to move toward energy self-sufficiency.

It took eight years (1961-69) for this country to conceive a plan to send people to the moon and then make it happen. If we had put in place a similar thrust in 1973, America could have been the leader today in solar and wind energy instead of China and Denmark. By dragging our feet, we lost an economic job-creating opportunity.

We can pass blame to the oil companies and to lack of leadership in this country, but what can and should we do from here?

Whether you believe in green energy, which contributes less carbon dioxide to the atmosphere, or energy independence so we and our allies are less dependent on foreign trouble spots, expanding the use of solar and wind energy makes sense. So does greater use of the new and safer Thorium Nuclear reactors that could reduce the amount of nuclear waste with much safer shut-down controls that would prevent the runaway meltdown that we fear from older plants.

Why is it that people who believe in less government regulations and less foreign entanglements would prefer to remain dependent on interstate and international oil and gas pipelines over having the added security of solar and wind near their homes? The main problem with wind and solar energy is storage. The Danes have worked on this problem. Elon Musk and others are improving battery technology to the point that we could envision a time when people unplug from the energy grid.

That would be power to the people and independence. Just a thought.

PART 10: OTHER

≈≈≈≈≈≈≈≈≈≈≈≈≈≈≈≈≈≈≈

GUN CONTROL

If you hate guns or love them, there's probably little that could change your mind, but consider this.

The Second Amendment states the right to bear arms in the context of "A well regulated Militia." This leaves some ambiguity in terms of the purpose and application of this amendment to the 21st century. At the time of this amendment, the nation was rural and militias were raised from the people who brought their own guns in support of the security of their state.

Today, states no longer raise militias. The closest analogy today would be to the National Guard, which supplies weapons in part so there will be uniformity and interchangeability of equipment. Nevertheless, the amendment does state that "the right of the people to keep and bear arms shall not be infringed." This clearly applies to actions by the Federal government. It's not clear that under the decentralized standards in effect at the time of enacting the Second Amendment and the importance of states' rights that there was any intent to restrict states and local governments from passing their own laws, though there are many who disagree.

As part of the debate, we should bear in mind one of the concerns faced by the Founding Fathers. They had just endured a long and difficult war of independence against Britain. It was only through the efforts of armed citizens that the war succeeded. There was a strong belief that only through an armed citizenry could the subjugation of the people be prevented.

It should be noted that Hitler disarmed citizens as did Stalin and every other dictator who sought to remove the ability of the people to resist tyranny. ISIS has also banned weapons except in the hands of their warriors. After gun control was established, each of these tyrants used their monopoly of power to kill civilians to impose their ideology and their rule.

It's not only tyrants we need to worry about. Paris has some of the strictest gun laws, which didn't prevent terrorists from bringing guns that they used to massacre civilians. Gun laws disarm the innocent. They may reduce guns in the hands of potential criminals, but determined criminals always find a way. If they can't find guns, they'll use knives, box-cutters, anything they can find. Are we to ban those as well?

If your motivation to ban guns is the number of deaths, consider that in 2013, there were 33,636 deaths by firearms in the United States. That was less than the number of deaths by vehicles. It should also be noted that there are far more guns than vehicles in this country and thus the incidence of death per vehicle is much higher than deaths per gun.

Should we ban private ownership of vehicles in order to save lives? Certainly airbags, seatbelts, and DUI tests aren't getting the job done. In addition, the number of people who died because of hospital mistakes has been estimated at 98 thousand, 180 thousand, and even higher each year. Should we close down all hospitals to save lives?

Those who seek to ban guns say the difference is that the only purpose of guns is to kill people. Gun advocates disagree by saying the purpose of guns is either for hunting or to protect the family, not for committing violence against others. The truth is that most gun owners do not kill people. Only one in 8,000 guns is involved in a death, a much lower incidence than for vehicles.

It should be noted that Switzerland has high gun ownership at about half of the U.S. rate, though they do have some gun restrictions. Although their gun ownership is much higher than Canada's, their gun violence is only slightly higher. That indicates that it isn't the number of guns itself that leads to violence.

In any case, to the extent that gun ownership is a right, those rights come with responsibilities that include gun safety. That means that those who do not practice gun safety or are not mentally capable of practicing gun safety and responsibility should not have those rights. Those with criminal backgrounds and mental/emotional problems that prevent them from showing due care with guns should be denied gun ownership. That is no different than denying the drivers' license to those who cannot demonstrate they can drive responsibly.

Some will argue that doing this starts down the slippery slope toward banning all guns. It very well might in the hands of a tyrant, but if gun advocates were to get behind keeping guns out of the hands of those who cannot exercise gun safety and responsibility, we could expect gun deaths to decline. Declining gun deaths would provide ammunition to gun advocates that they are showing civic responsibility and having a favorable effect on reducing gun violence.

Instead of acting defensively, perhaps gun advocates could get ahead of this and represent the voice of gun safety and responsibility. Find ways on the state if not Federal level to put in place reasonable practices and guidelines that would improve gun safety and reduce guns in the hands of people who don't or can't act responsibly. Lead the way by tackling gun violence while protecting gun rights.

POSTSCRIPT

Thank you for joining me in exploring behind the candidates' mantras and promises. Regrettably, many of these issues are complex and candidates prefer to simplify. The media pushes them in that direction with their grab at sound-bites. I hope this journey has provided some insight into the campaigns.

We've encountered some uncommon sense along the way, situations where history does not support prevailing opinion. If you were looking for simple answers, I apologize. Despite what many candidates would have you believe, simple solutions don't exist. There really is no free lunch; someone always has to pay and usually not those the candidates promise. On the other hand, we can't solve problems until we properly identify them. Hopefully these discussions can help.

The inconvenient truth is that governments have less tools and controls to get it right than people would like. Because of side-effects, governments have far more chances to get it wrong. That frustrates voters. Candidates who tell the truth get shut down. Only informed citizens can push to change this, demanding better from candidates and the media that covers them.

Rather than despair that the government can't solve more of our problems without side-effects, let's work together to get our candidates to lay out the consequences of their actions so we can make better choices.

One takeaway I would leave you with is that wages began to stagnate when the economy could no longer absorb an increase in labor participation and immigration. Outsourcing has also been a cause. One solution would be to adopt a Value Added Tax (VAT) as many of our trading partners have in order to level the international playing field. The other would be to slow immigration (legal and illegal) to around 500,000 per year, an equivalent rate to what it was the last time wages were growing.

This journey was never intended to cover every possible myth and misinformation or deal with every side-effect of public policies. The goal was to point out some misconceptions that often get oversimplified in our discussions of important issues. Our belief is that better informed citizens can make better choices. We encourage readers to keep digging.

It has been the author's intent to be as factual and informative as possible. If you find any information you believe is not accurate or that you would like clarified or further developed, please contact the author at Tomas.Payne76@gmail.com.

BIBLIOGRAPHY

GOVERNMENTAL SOURCES

1. BEA.gov "Current Dollar and Real Gross Domestic Product." n.d. Web. 1 Mar. 2016. <https://www.bea.gov/national/xls/gdplev.xls>
2. BEA.gov "Real Gross Domestic Product (GDPC1). US Bureau of Economic Analysis." n.d. Web. 1 Mar. 2016. <http://www.bea.gov/national/#gdp>
3. BLS.gov "A Century of Family Budgets in the United States." May 2001. Web. 1 Mar. 2016. <http://www.bls.gov/opub/mlr/2001/05/art3full.pdf>
4. BLS.gov "The Employment Situation December 2015" n.d. Web. 1 Mar. 2016. <http://www.bls.gov/news.release/pdf/empsit.pdf>
5. CBO.gov "The Budget and Economic Outlook: 2016 to 2026." 25 Jan. 2016. Web. 1 Mar. 2016. <http://www.cbo.gov/publication/51129>
6. CBO.gov "The Distribution of Household Income and Federal Taxes, 2011." 18 Nov. 2014. Web. 1 Mar. 2016. <http://www.cbo.gov/publication/49440>
7. Census.gov "Current Population Survey Annual Social and Economic Supplement (CPS ASEC). Selected Characteristics of Households in 2014 (hinc01_1)." n.d. Web. 1 Mar. 2016. <https://www.census.gov/search-results.html?q=hinc01_1&search.x=0&search.y=0&search=s

8. Census.gov "Current Population Survey Annual Social andEconomic Supplement (CPS ASEC)." n.d. Web. 1 Mar. 2016. <https://www.census.gov/hhes/www/poverty/publications/pubs-cps.html>
9. Census.gov "2014 Household Income Table of Contents." n.d. Web. 9 Mar 2016. <https://www.census.gov/hhes/www/cpstables/032015/hhinc/toc.htm>
10. Census.gov "America's Families and Living Arrangements (hh4)." n.d. Web. 1 Mar. 2016. <https://www.census.gov/search-results.html?page=1&stateGeo=none&searchtype=web&cssp=SERP&q=hh4&search.x=0&search.y=0&search=submit>
11. Census.gov "Health Insurance Coverage in the United States 2014." Sept. 2015. Web. 1 Mar. 2016. <https://www.census.gov/content/dam/Census/library/publications/2015/demo/p60-253.pdf>
12. CIA.gov "The World Factbook - GDP per capita purchasing parity basis." n.d. Web. 1 Mar. 2016. <https://www.cia.gov/library/publications/the-world-factbook/fields/2004.html>
13. Climate.NASA.gov "Graphic: The Relentless Rise of Carbon Dioxide." n.d. Web. 1 Mar. 2016. <http://climate.nasa.gov/climate_resources/24/>
14. CMS.gov (Centers for Medicare & Medicaid Services) "Historical." n.d. Web. 1 Mar. 2015 <https://www.cms.gov/research-statistics-data-and-systems/statistics-trends-and-reports/nationalhealthexpenddata/nationalhealthaccountshistorical.html>
15. Data.BLS.gov "Manufacturing Labor Productivity." n.d. Web. 1 Mar. 2016. <http://data.bls.gov/pdq/SurveyOutputServlet>
16. DHS.gov "Annual Number of U.S. Legal Permanent Residents: Fiscal Years 1820 to 2013"n.d. Web. 9 Mar 2016 <http://www.dhs.gov/files/statistics/publications/yearbook.shtm>

17. FederalReserve.gov "How Much Student Debt Is Out There?" 7 Aug. 2015. Web. 1 Mar. 2016. <http://www.federalreserve.gov/econresdata/notes/feds-notes/2015/how-much-student-debt-is-out-there-20150807.html>.
18. Future.State.gov "Smoot-Hawley Tariff." n.d. Web. 1 Mar. 2016. <http://future.state.gov/when/timeline/1921_timeline/smoot_tariff.html>
19. GISS.NASA.gov "Earth's Climate History: Implications for Tomorrow." July 2011. Web. 1 Mar. 2016. <http://www.giss.nasa.gov/research/briefs/hansen_15/>
20. IRS.gov "SOI Tax Stats - Individual Statistical Tables by Size of Adjusted Gross Income." n.d. Web. 1 Mar. 2016. <https://www.irs.gov/uac/SOI-Tax-Stats---Individual-Statistical-Tables-by-Size-of-Adjusted-Gross-Income>
21. IRS.gov "SOI Tax Stats-Estate Tax Statistics Filing Year Table 1." n.d. Web. 8 Mar. 2016. <https://www.irs.gov/uac/SOI-Tax-Stats-Estate-Tax-Statistics-Filing-Year-Table-1>
22. Medicaid.gov "How Medicare is Funded." n.d. Web. 1 Mar. 2016. <https://www.medicare.gov/about-us/how-medicare-is-funded/medicare-funding.html>
23. Medicaid.gov "Medicaid Information by Topic." n.d. Web. 1 Mar. 2016. <https://www.medicaid.gov/medicaid-chip-program-information/by-topics/by-topic.html>
24. Mosisa, Abraham and Steven Hipple "Trends in Labor Force Participation in the United States." Oct. 2016 Web. 1 Mar. 2016. <http://www.bls.gov/opub/mlr/2006/10/art3full.pdf>
25. NCDC.NOAA.gov (National Oceanic and Atmospheric Administration) "Abrupt Climate Change." n.d. Web. 1 Mar. 2016. <http://www.ncdc.noaa.gov/paleo/ctl/clisci10k.html>
26. SocialSecurity.gov "Primary Insurance Amount." n.d. Web. 1 Mar. 2016. <https://www.socialsecurity.gov/OACT/COLA/piaformula.html>
27. SSA.gov "Life Expectancy for Social Security." n.d. Web. 1 Mar. 2016. <https://www.ssa.gov/history/lifeexpect.html>

28. SSA.gov "Summary of Provisions that Would Change the Social Security Program." 20 January 2016. Web. 1 Mar. 2016. <https://www.ssa.gov/oact/solvency/provisions/summary.pdf>
29. SSA.gov "Trends in the Social Security and Supplemental Security Income Disability Programs." n.d. Web. 1 Mar. 2016. <https://www.ssa.gov/policy/docs/chartbooks/disability_trends/overview.html>
30. U.S. Census Bureau, Population Division. Table 1. Monthly Population Estimates for the United States: April 1, 2010 to December 1, 2016 (NA-EST2015-01) Dec. 2015.
31. WhiteHouse.gov "Historical Tables." n.d. Web. 1 Mar. 2016. <http://www.whitehouse.gov/omb/budget/Historicals/>

NON-GOVERNMENTAL SOURCES

32. AgClassRoom.org "Historical Timeline." n.d. Web. 1 Mar. 2016. <https://www.agclassroom.org/gan/timeline/1900.htm>
33. AstroBio.net "How Earth's Orbital Shift Shaped the Sahara." 20 Dec. 2010. Web. 1 Mar. 2016. <http://www.astrobio.net/news-exclusive/how-earths-orbital-shift-shaped-the-sahara/>
34. Bivens, Josh and Elise Gould, Lawrence Mishel, and Heidi Shierholz. "Raising America's Pay." EPI.org 2 June 2014. Web. 1 Mar. 2016. <http://www.epi.org/publication/raising-americas-pay/>
35. ChinaHighlights.com "Chinese Ethnic Groups." n.d. Web. 1 Mar. 2016. <http://www.chinahighlights.com/travelguide/nationality/>
36. Civil-War.net "Results from the 1860 Census." n.d. Web. 1 Mar. 2016. <http://www.civil-war.net/pages/1860_census.html>
37. CNN.com "Death and Guns in the USA: The story in six graphs." 3 Oct. 2015. Web. 1 Mar. 2016. <http://www.cnn.com/2015/10/03/us/gun-deaths-united-states/>
38. Demos.org "It Takes Nearly $8 Million to Join Wealthiest One-Percent." 19 Sept. 2014. Web. 1 Mar. 2016. <http://www.demos.org/blog/9/19/14/it-takes-nearly-8-million-join-wealthiest-one-percent>

39. GGDC.net. "Historical Statistics of the World Economy: 1-2008 AD." n.d. Web. 9 Mar. 2016. <www.ggdc.net/maddison/Historical_Statistics/horizontal-file_02-2010.xls>
40. GlobalRichList.com n.d. Web. 1 Mar. 2016. <http://www.globalrichlist.com/>
41. Hodge, Scott A. "Who Are America's Millionaires?" TaxFoundation.org 15 June 2012. Web. 1 Mar. 2016. <http://taxfoundation.org/article/who-are-americas-millionaires>
42. Lundeen, Andrew and Scott A. Hodge. "Income Tax Code Spans More than 70,000 Pages." TaxFoundation.org 23 Oct 2013. Web. 1 Mar. 2016. <http://taxfoundation.org/blog/income-tax-code-spans-more-70000-pages>
43. Lundeen, Andrew. "France's 75 Percent Tax Rate Offers Lesson in Revenue Estimating." TaxFoundation.org 28 May 2014. Web. 1 Mar. 2016. <http://taxfoundation.org/blog/france-s-75-percent-tax-rate-offers-lesson-revenue-estimating>
44. Lundeen, Andrew. "The Top 1 Percent Pays More in Taxes than the Bottom 90 Percent." TaxFoundation.org 7 Jan. 2014. Web. 1 Mar. 2016. <http://taxfoundation.org/blog/top-1-percent-pays-more-taxes-bottom-90-percent>
45. Moorhead, Molly. "Bernie Sanders Says Walmart Heirs Own More Wealth then Bottom 40 percent of Americans." Politifact.com 31 July 2012. Web. 1 Mar. 2016. <http://www.politifact.com/truth-o-meter/statements/2012/jul/31/bernie-s/sanders-says-walmart-heirs-own-more-wealth-bottom-/>
46. PewHispanic.org "Unauthorized Immigrant Population Trends for States, Birth Countries and Regions." 11 Dec. 2014. Web. 1 Mar. 2016. <http://www.pewhispanic.org/2014/12/11/unauthorized-trends/>
47. PewResearch.org "Key Takeaways on U.S. Immigration Past, Present and Future." 28 Sept. 2015. Web. 1 Mar. 2016. <http://www.pewresearch.org/fact-tank/2015/09/28/key-takeaways-on-u-s-immigration-past-present-and-future/>

48. Politifact.com "Bernie Sanders Says Income Inequality is Widest Since the 1920s." 18 June 2015. Web. 1 Mar. 2016. <http://www.politifact.com/truth-o-meter/statements/2015/jun/18/bernie-s/bernie-sanders-says-income-inequality-widest-1920s/>
49. Politifact.com "Medicare and Social Security: What you paid compared with what you get." 1 Feb. 2013. Web. 1 Mar. 2016. <http://www.politifact.com/truth-o-meter/article/2013/feb/01/medicare-and-social-security-what-you-paid-what-yo/>
50. Research.StLouis.org "All Employees: Manufacturing." 4 Mar. 2016. Web. 7 Mar. 2016. <https://research.stlouisfed.org/fred2/series/MANEMP>
51. Research.StLouisFed.org "Commercial Banks in the U.S. (USNUM)." n.d. Web. 1 Mar. 2016. <https://research.stlouisfed.org/fred2/series/USNUM/downloaddata>
52. Smith, Adam, An Inquiry Into The Nature And Causes Of The Wealth Of Nations, The Project Gutenberg Etext, April 2002
53. Statista.com "Number of Health Insurance Employees in the US from 1960 to 2014." n.d. Web. 1 Mar. 2016. <http://www.statista.com/statistics/194229/number-of-health-insurance-employees-in-the-us-since-1960/>
54. Stats.Areppim.com "2015 World Billionaires Worth 10 Percent o Gross World Product." 25 Apr. 2015. Web. 1 Mar. 2016. <http://stats.areppim.com/archives/insight_billionaires_2015.pdf>
55. TaxFoundation.org "U.S. Federal Individual Income Tax Rates History, 1862-2013." n.d. Web. 1 Mar. 2016. <http://taxfoundation.org/article/us-federal-individual-income-tax-rates-history-1913-2013-nominal-and-inflation-adjusted-brackets>
56. TaxPolicyCenter.org "Historical Corporate Top Tax Rate and Bracket: 1909-2014" 2 Dec. 2015. Web. 1 Mar. 2016. <http://www.taxpolicycenter.org/taxfacts/displayafact.cfm?Docid=65>
57. TaxPolicyCenter.org "Who Doesn't Pay Federal Taxes?" n.d. Web. 1 Mar. 2016. <http://www.taxpolicycenter.org/taxtopics/federal-taxes-households.cfm>

58. Trends.Collegeboard.org "Average Published Undergraduate Charges by Sector, 2015-16." n.d. Web. 1 Mar. 2016. <http://trends.collegeboard.org/college-pricing/figures-tables/average-published-undergraduate-charges-s
59. UCAR.edu "Global Climate Change." n.d. Web. 1 Mar. 2016. <https://www.ucar.edu/learn/1_4_1.htm>
60. Umhoefer, Dave. "Did FDR Oppose Collective Bargaining For Government Workers?" Politifact.com 13 Aug. 2013. Web. 1 Mar. 2016. <http://www.politifact.com/wisconsin/statements/2013/aug/13/scott-walker/Did-FDR-oppose-collective-bargaining-for-governmen/>
61. USInflationCalculator.com "Historical Inflation Rates: 1914-2016." n.d. Web. 1 Mar. 2016. <http://www.usinflationcalculator.com/inflation/historical-inflation-rates/>
62. USNews.com "Outsourcing to China Cost U.S. 3.2 Million Jobs Since 2001." 11 Dec. 2014. Web. 1 Mar. 2016. <http://www.usnews.com/news/blogs/data-mine/2014/12/11/outsourcing-to-china-cost-us-32-million-jobs-since-2001>
63. Wikipedia.org "JusSoli (Birthright Citizenship)." n.d. Web. 1 Mar. 2016. <https://en.wikipedia.org/wiki/Jus_soli>
64. Wikipedia.org "Smoot-Hawley Tariff Act." n.d. Web. 1 Mar. 2016. <https://en.wikipedia.org/wiki/Smoot%E2%80%93Hawley_Tariff_Act>
65. Yamamoto, Dale H. *HealthCostInstitute.org* "Health Care Costs-From Birth to Death." June 2013. Web. 1 Mar. 2016. <http://www.healthcostinstitute.org/files/Age-Curve-Study_0.pdf>

AUTHOR

Tomas Payne is a CPA and has an MBA in Finance, a BS in Political Science and over 30 years of business experience. He is a longtime student of business, the ever-entertaining field of economics, and of the political shell game.

Find out more about the author and his work at WhatTheyDontTellU.wordpress.com.

CPSIA information can be obtained
at www.ICGtesting.com
Printed in the USA
BVOW06s1334170117
473717BV00012B/81/P